A Guy's Guide
to Shoes

For Bettina

I would like to thank everyone who has helped me
during the work on this book.

© h.f.ullmann publishing GmbH
Original title: *Schuh Guide für Männer*
Original ISBN: 978-3-8480-0293-1

Project management: Lars Pietzschmann
Design, typesetting, and layout: Erill Fritz, Berlin
Production department: Sabine Vogt

Cover photo: © erill.fritz.fotografien
End-papers: Cove & Co., Düsseldorf

© for the English edition: h.f.ullmann publishing GmbH

Translation from German by JMS Books llp
in association with Malcolm Garrard and cbdesign

Overall responsibility for production: h.f.ullmann publishing GmbH,
Potsdam, Germany

Printed in China, 2013

ISBN 978-3-8480-0294-8

10 9 8 7 6 5 4 3 2 1
X IX VIII VII VI V IV III II I

www.ullmann-publishing.com
newsletter@ullmann-publishing.com

Bernhard Roetzel

A Guy's Guide to Shoes

h.f.ullmann

Foreword

Women are often said to have a thing about shoes, and it is certainly true that a lot of women enjoy buying them and would be happy to indulge in this pleasure on a daily basis. It is equally true, however, that men are often no less fascinated by their footwear, and I would even go so far as to say that men pursue this passion with more single-minded dedication than women. This applies both to the financial outlay they incur and the space in the home they devote to their shoes: while a cedarwood shoe rack will do initially, eventually you end up needing a whole shoe cupboard or even a walk-in wardrobe. This doesn't just apply to fans of fine, welted footwear; sneaker fans and cowboy boot aficionados often require whole rooms in which to collect their treasures and the boxes that they came in. Shoes fascinate men more than any other part of their wardrobe.

When I talk to people at book signings, it often seems to be the case that the gentlemen with the greatest interest in high-end shoes are those wearing clothes that might otherwise suggest they attach little or no importance to outward appearances. People wearing sweatshirts and jeans suddenly want to know everything about hand-made shoes, such as where they can be bought and how much they might expect to pay for them. There is clearly a place for good shoes in every wardrobe. Few men are required to wear a suit any more, but pretty much everyone can find a use for some handstitched lace-ups, so I often hear the comment: "If I were ever to have something made to measure, it would be a pair of shoes."

Even those with no special interest in shoes will at least want footwear that is the right size. No one looks good in an ill-fitting suit; the wearer probably doesn't feel good either and it creates a poor impression. However, badly fitted shoes are painful and can even cause damage to your feet over time. Even if you can do without dress shoes since you don't wear tails, you will need something to put on your feet; with going barefoot not really an option for most of us, there's no running away from the need for shoes.

Bernhard Roetzel

Shoes: the

Footwear is a matter of interest to everyone—even to people whose shoes you privately believe to be in dreadful taste. At least, this is the impression I have formed from countless conversations before and after lectures, at book signings and receptions, and at private parties. Men are concerned about their shoes, be they sandals, biker boots, sneakers, handstitched lace-ups, or flip-flops, and they want to share this concern. Ideally—apparently—with me.

As a writer, I am expected to show an interest and maintain a certain neutrality, and for some people I even seem to occupy the same position as a father confessor. People rarely speak so openly about shoes as they do with me: not with the sales staff, who are usually not to be trusted since, ultimately, they are trying to sell something. Not with their partner, who is either too close or has a taste in shoes that is too far removed. Not with friends or colleagues, with whom most men would find it embarrassing to talk about shoes.

This disinclination to admit an interest in shoes has a number of causes. The view that it is unmanly to take an interest in clothes in general, and thus in shoes in particular, is still widespread, and such an enthusiasm is often suppressed since little importance is attached to clothing as a rule. There are so many other important topics to discuss, such as healthy eating, global warming, or world hunger—who wants to have a serious conversation about never having found a pair of shoes that didn't hurt after a couple of hours?

Foundations of Style

Shoe problems are very personal, involving pain that only the individual can feel and aesthetic suffering that the wearer feels they cannot share.

Inadequate advice in shoe shops often means that people never find shoes that fit really well or support and cradle the foot. People may suffer from excess sweating, resulting in embarrassment and even impinging on their immediate surroundings with foot odor, because ignorance has led them to choose the wrong materials for their shoes and socks. People may be doomed to feel ill at ease in their shoes, as they fit neither their feet nor their personality.

"You see only what you know"—I often use this quotation from Goethe in lectures, and it also applies to shoes of course. Only when I know what shape my foot is can I find a shoe to fit that shape. Only when I have found out about the materials from which shoes are made can I find a material that will let my foot breathe and won't suffocate it. Only when I have learned about the most important classic shoes and understood their significance in the different worlds of fashion and style can I find a shoe that suits my personality and what I wish to express with my clothes.

Whether it's a stitched and welted lace-up like these from Cove & Co. or a sneaker from Footlocker—the right shoe finishes the outfit.

Der Schuhmacher.

THE HISTORY OF SHOES IS AS MUCH ABOUT 1980s
FASHION AS IT IS ABOUT THE MIDDLE AGES.

The History of Shoes

Fashion history is of interest to very few people. Who wants to know what sort of sandals they wore in Ancient Rome or what was all the rage in 16th-century Venice? But the story of fashion is not always about such remote eras—what happened in the early 20th century is fashion history too and, depending on how old you are, you might think the 1980s a distant era as well. Indeed, the styles of previous decades are still around today, wielding an influence in the form of retro fashions and the current trend for "vintage" shoes.

Stroll through a fashion museum or shoe collection where you can see real shoes from previous eras close up, or handle and try on old footwear at flea markets or in thrift stores, and the distance between today and yesterday—or even centuries ago—melts away. You can suddenly imagine how people a few generations before us lived, loved, and worked wearing their shoes. In Europe, fashion was a force that was enthusing, enlivening, and animating people as early as the 15th century, and even at that time, the changing fashions were an expression of a dynamic society in constant flux.

Shoe fashions are a truly visual sign of their times, revealing much about the circumstances of people's lives: shoes were polished, patched, and sometimes even passed down from generation to generation. People saved up and worked hard for shoes, but they were also a luxury item for the rich and powerful; kings, princes, and wealthy merchants would wear shoes which cost several times the annual earnings of a simple peasant. Exotic materials for uppers and soles were brought from distant lands and crafted into real works of art by skilled artisans.

The cult of the fine shoe is extremely old—and rebellion against prevailing customs and the older generation, as expressed through shoe choice, is just as old. Fashion history is social history and the history of humanity itself, and as such is just as relevant as the history of art or architecture.

Shoes have always been a sought-after aspect of fashion on which people were prepared to spend a lot of money. In addition, shoes were also a statement about belonging to a particular status and rank.

The Looks of the 20th Century

Much is made of revivals in fashion; first the 1960s are back, then the 1980s, now it's the turn of the 1950s. But this presupposes that a particular style can be ascribed to each decade, and that is a misconception. Of course it's true that there are fashions which are neatly limited to a single decade and which can

20s

Men's fashion reaches its apotheosis in the 1920s, with style initiatives that began at the end of the 19th century coming to fruition. The various elements of an outfit are balanced, with the fashionable turnups seen on pants, and extended collar shapes and shoe silhouettes merely small deviations from this stylish sense of proportion. Boots and low shoes are equally favored.

30s

Fashion is taken to extremes in the 1930s, perhaps reflecting the great tensions of the decade. Pants, turnups, and lapels are suddenly extremely wide. The shoulders of jackets extend far beyond those of the wearer, and doublebreasted suits are popular. Hats have wide brims. Boots lose the fight against low shoes, which now rule the roost.

40s

The Second World War casts its shadow almost everywhere during the first half of the 1940s, and shortages and great want mean that fashion is last on the list of priorities. Once the war is over, old clothes are worn or altered to fit in the countries most affected by the fighting, and new clothes are often handmade. The general populace wears simple shoes of low quality. By contrast, the United States experiences great prosperity and sees shoe styles becoming more sporty.

50s

The fashion of the 1950s has two aspects; on the one hand, these are still times of shortages and want, but it is also a decade of innovation, with the old and the new, the young and the old in conflict with one another. While many fashions revert back to the classics, young people are beginning to carve out a place for themselves and their clothing. Shoes start off with round toes, but toward the subsequently be seen as typical for the period, or indeed actually are typical; but there has never been a decade when everyone wore only the styles from that particular era—it's more the case that people wear clothes from different decades at the same time.

To borrow from the writer Gregor von Rezzori, you could describe this as "epoch creep"—people don't throw out their entire wardrobe on New Year's Day of a new decade, they hang on to things and even ten years later may be wearing the same shoes and fabrics. The fashions that are claimed to be the defining style of an era are mostly those that arise in the middle or toward the end of a decade and may have only really become commonplace by the start of the next decade: "typical 1970s clothes," such as wide-legged bell-bottom jeans, were worn by some well into the 1980s, for example.

end of the decade they get more and more pointed. The shoe trade also discovers young people.

60s

The showdown between the generations erupts in the 1960s, when the conflict that has been brewing in the postwar years finally boils over. The differences in fashion between the generations get wider, as seen in the contrasts on the street, with older men and pensioners in hats, coats, and suits, and young men with long hair, beards, and sideburns who sport leather jackets, jeans, and sandals.

70s

The early 1970s continue the themes of the 1960s by other means; the pretty floral prints of the 1970s seem twice as striking in retrospect as fashion and press images are now all in color. In the early 1960s, the Beatles seem cool and muted in black and white; Jimi Hendrix looks psychedelic in color. Shoe toecaps are rounded off, soles and heels are jacked up, and seams on pants are more prominent.

80s

As a reaction to the colorful 1960s and 70s, the 1980s have been dismissed as the "decade of black." This is not true of the whole period, of course; the end of the decade is characterized by extreme neon colors, but designer fashion in the 1980s does have a particular preference for black, the "anticolor." Sneakers continue their triumphal march but an awareness of classic shoes is beginning to grow.

90s

The 1990s are the least homogenous decade of the 20th century. There are plenty of individual trends in designer fashion—minimalism, deconstruction, historicism, streetwear, and grunge—but it is difficult to isolate a definitive look for the decade. It is possibly best defined by the color brown, representing both nature but also indecision.

From Boots
Shoes Get

People in the fashion industry have been talking about the "casualization" of fashion for a number of years, as "casual looks" replace more formal outfits. The causes are obvious: people in industrialized countries have more and more free time, itself reason enough to be choosing more leisurewear, and are also becoming less inclined to put on suits, which are now considered uncomfortable and impractical. This tendency has of course carried over to footwear; leisure shoes such as sports shoes, sandals, health shoes, bathing shoes, walking boots, and clogs are taking the place once occupied by ordinary street shoes right up to the 1950s.

It is difficult to say exactly when the casualization of fashion began, but it is safe to say that the phenomenon has its roots somewhere in the last 100 to 150 years. For one thing, the existence of leisure shoes presupposes the existence of free time, not to mention the material means to acquire shoes purely dedicated to such time. It can be assumed, therefore, that the first leisure shoes were worn by the rich, including the nobility, manufacturers, merchants, and well-off artisans. As productive work was the most important daytime activity for the majority of men (with the exception of a few extremely wealthy individuals), it was most likely upper-class women, excluded by convention from earning a living, who had leisure time—and thus leisure shoes.

(Left) The laced boot, like this one by Shoepassion, was the forerunner of the low shoe. (Right) Sneakers, such as this one by Künzli, are for many the epitome of shoes for everyday wear.

to Sneakers: Casual

The popularity of a number of different kinds of sports grew at the end of the 19th century, which meant that new sports shoes were developed or existing footwear was adapted. At the same time, the increasing spread of industrialization meant that cheap shoes could be produced in greater quantities. Consumption began to drive production and the industry soon learned to produce affordable goods to satisfy the needs of the general populace. Free time, which was still extremely scarce, was generally used to recover from the exertions of the week, but was also used for leisure activities, of course: dancing and drinking, sports and hiking, "intellectual improvement," and reading. Leisure clothes and leisure

shoes also helped to separate this sphere from the world of paid work. The shop coat went back on its nail on Saturday evening, and out came the blazer, with matching "Saturday night special" shoes. Casualization really took off in the 1950s—after the Second World War there was an almost insatiable desire for renewal, a strong urge to strip away the past, as well as considerable enthusiasm for modern technology. This was all perfectly symbolized by American clothes, which have been worn by generations of young people all around the globe ever since.

Lisy Christl on Shoes

"
My job as a costume designer means that I have some influence on the shoes an actor wears. People talk a lot about shoes but rarely notice them actively, which is a good thing. If the story permits, I am always happy to get good, handsewn, and welted shoes into the spotlight.
"

Lisy Christl, a native of Munich now living in Berlin, has a very special perspective on fashion. In her job, she has to make clothes "speak" without words, but also support the words that are spoken. She is an expert at this, which is why she was nominated for an Oscar for Best Costume Design in 2012.

Swing or Music

There's a close connection between shoes and youth culture. When Carl Perkins wrote the now legendary song "Blue Suede Shoes" in 1955, he created what amounts to a hymn to the rock 'n' roll lifestyle. Blue suede shoes have become synonymous with music from the 1950s and the rebellion it expressed, but even though British teddy boys in the 1970s liked to wear crepe-soled shoes made of blue velour leather, so-called "creepers," this was a style of shoe that teenagers never really wore in the 1950s; instead, they tended to wear simple canvas gym pumps, two-tone shoes, or penny loafers.

There has always been conflict between the generations in some form or other, but modern conditions cannot be translated back to the Ancient World, the Middle Ages, the Renaissance, or the Romantic period—social conventions, religious affiliations, family ties, life expectancy, and material wealth are all so varied during the periods mentioned that comparisons are impossible to draw. What did youthful rebellion in Ancient Rome look like? Or in medieval Nuremberg? Decidedly different from America in the 1950s. Although people like to imagine that it was the case, no rebellion took place among the broad mass of American young people—Frank Sinatra, the biggest music idol of the 1940s, and Elvis Presley, the biggest star of the 1950s, annoyed a few parents with their singing and their appearance, but in their early years they lived extremely conventional lives. Real rebellion was not expressed until the music of the 1960s, and there was of course footwear to match. We have to mention the Beatles' boots, although these belong to a period when the band's fashions were more conventional; the respectable middle classes found the platform shoes and sandals worn by rockers from the late 1960s to the end of the 1970s far more shocking.

Laced army boots and work boots from England took to the fashion stage with punks like the Sex Pistols, who had begun

The Fender Telecaster is as much a symbol of rock 'n' roll as Ace label jeans by the Berlin designer Annika Graalfs.

Rock 'n' Roll: and Shoes

to appear on television screens in their new style of footwear and clothes decorated with safety pins, while rappers and hip-hop artists sported basketball boots or other kinds of sneakers in preference—never laced up but always spotlessly clean. In contrast, the worn canvas gym shoes favored by grunge musicians would simply never have been cool enough. Such are the ties between music and shoes.

Shoes and Youth Cults

Cowboys and the Wild West

The myth of the American cowboy fascinates men all over the world, and they can live it out in jeans, a Stetson, and cowboy boots.

Beatniks and Existentialists

The American beatniks wore leather jackets, lumberjack shirts, and rough boots, while their French counterparts, the existentialists, preferred black, especially when matched with desert boots or penny loafers.

Hipsters and Zoots

Wide double-breasted zoot suits and baggy pants, large-brimmed hats, and wide ties marked out the hip jazz fans of the 1940s and 1950s, and two-tone spectator shoes were part of the look.

Surfers

The surfers of the 1950s wore Hawaiian shirts, shorts, thongs, canvas gym shoes, or penny loafers, although nowadays they prefer T-shirts and Vans.

Preppy

The preppy look is sporty, clean, and traditional, featuring button-down shirts, polo shirts, blazers, chinos, and a marked preference for deck shoes or penny loafers.

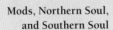

Rockabilly, Teddyboys, and Psychobilly

Rockabilly fans favored denim, rough boots, and leather jackets, while devotees of psychobilly opted for military boots or creepers with extremely thick soles. The first British teddy boys were elegant, with frock coats, vests, and crepe-soled shoes.

Mods, Northern Soul, and Southern Soul

Tight-fitting suits, army parkas, Eton jackets, or even duffle coats epitomize this look. Loafers or lace-up winklepickers or Beatle boots are often paired with white socks.

Skinheads
The original skinheads had a different image from today's closely cropped right-wing extremists. Jeans with turn-ups and suspenders, windbreakers, and polo shirts were all matched with Dr. Martens boots.

Rockers and Headbangers
A black leather jacket, jeans, and biker boots form the basis of a rocker, headbanger, or greaser's everyday wardrobe.

Hippies and Grunge
Hippies cultivate long hair and beards and sport T-shirts, jeans, and sandals, while grunge fans prefer canvas gym shoes.

Skaters and Snowboarders
Skaters tend to buy their streetwear in XXL sizes and always choose sneakers for their feet, such as these by Converse. Snowboarders need to wear dedicated boots when actually on the piste, of course.

Punks

The punks of the 1970s and their scrappy outfits of leather jacket, jeans, T-shirts, and army boots, all decorated with safety pins, came as a shock, both to the respectable middle classes and the hippies.

The Great Outdoors

While turnover in ordinary fashion shops has been stagnating, outdoors specialists have been enjoying significant growth in sales. Nature fans love clothing and footwear that can be called "functional," and the Tewa sandal is their calling card.

Eco-warrior

The eco-warrior look is an environmentally aware and health-conscious version of hippy fashion, in other words handknit pullovers, dungarees, and health clogs.

Techno and Rave

The techno and rave scene spawned countless outfits, but a typical look for the late 1980s would include puffer jackets, T-shirts, hooded tops, and suede wallabees.

Shoes Are History

As banal a statement as it may be, people have probably always worn shoes. However, what shape they were and what materials they were made of depended largely on what stage of development their civilization had attained, the climate, and of course on fashion—and the fact that even the simplest sandals were decorated in some way places them under the heading "fashion item".

Sometimes the shoe was the only item of clothing worn; outer garments could be discarded in hot weather, but the foot would always need protection from stones and thorns. From the earliest times, shoes and boots were fashioned to provide their wearers with effective protection in cold regions, and anyone who has visited a shoe museum will generally be impressed by the range of different forms of footwear used around the world. That said, all the exhibits on show can usually be boiled down to only five basic shapes: sandals, moccasins, shoes, boots, and slippers.

Sandals consist of a sole that is attached to the foot, ankle, or toe with bands, straps, or an upper section. For moccasins, also known as "opankas," the sole is wrapped around the foot from underneath, folded up and then closed at the top using either a stitched seam or a lace. A shoe is made by combining a sole and an upper, sometimes with a heel, while a boot is made by continuing the upper portion along the leg. A slipper consists of a closed upper section and a sole. These basic forms can of course be combined with one another.

European shoe fashion begins with the Greek and Roman sandals of ancient times, which we know principally from paintings. The Middle Ages chiefly favored crakows, shoes with extended toes, which were worn by the upper classes; it was the half-boot for the ordinary folk, who would otherwise often run about barefoot, especially in summer. The crakow is an early example of how we adopted fashions from other countries, being inspired by footwear from the Orient. The crakow was augmented with wooden undersoles and uppers which were intended to protect the soft shoes themselves. Peasants and artisans would button or lace half-boots whose shapes seem absolutely timeless, almost modern.

The crakow finally fell out of fashion at the end of the 15th century. A wider shape was called for, and the so-called "cow-mouth shoe" became popular. Unlike the crakow, the shoe was the same shape for both feet. Heels were still unknown and only began to feature around 1600, at which point the modern-style shoe, which to this day consists of an upper, a sole, and a heel, could begin to develop.

Riding boots became more popular as a fashion accessory from the mid-16th century onward, as the original function of the riding boot—to protect the leg—became less and less important. Riding boots were so heavy and stiff in the Middle Ages that it would have been impossible to run in them, but by the 18th century they had become soft and comfortable.

By the end of the 19th century, shoes had acquired asymmetric shapes; this of course increased the workload for manufacturers, and a good last became increasingly important. A greater degree of variety in footwear styles was ensured by the accelerating spread of mass production during the 19th century; a multitude of different shapes and styles is a phenomenon not confined to our times. The general tendency, however, was that men's shoes were to become less striking and their elegance was circumscribed by their functionality.

The 20th century dawned with conservative shoe fashions, but the two world wars ushered in and accelerated developments that would otherwise probably have taken much longer to crystallize. Low boots were the norm for

gentlemen until the First World War, with the half-shoe making its presence felt after 1918. The United States and its fashions had a greater influence on Europe after the Second World War, which is a tendency that has continued to this day.

Leisure and youth fashions finally asserted their dominance in the 1960s—traditional menswear was now considered old-fashioned and was largely abandoned as a result. Elegance was decried as snobbishness and as such it stood in the way of the predominant ideal of equality. Although the classic men's shoe was not entirely swept away, it now occupied only a small niche with most men choosing instead to enjoy wearable sportswear or comfortable shoes.

Making Shoes

What makes a good shoe? The last on which it is made or the look of the shoe? Most people today would say it is a combination of the two. It is often said that you have to suffer to be beautiful—and there are indeed plenty of women who will subject themselves to painful feet to achieve a particular look—but there are few who would suggest that entirely uncomfortable and unsuitable footwear makes for a "good" shoe, however beautiful.

The majority would be just as unlikely to place the emphasis entirely on the correct last and the health of the foot, since far too many so-called "health shoes" look rather unappealing.

The history of humanity encompasses the widest variety of footwear, yet very few actual shoes have survived from before the most recent past (researchers have otherwise had to rely on images, texts, and sculptures), so while we may attempt to get our heads around the shape of historic shoes, we cannot really get our toes inside them. We can, however, assume that it has always been important to people that shoes did not pinch or hurt, and the original examples that have survived from the Middle Ages and the Renaissance do not appear to fit any worse than their modern counterparts.

The division of shoes into "left" and "right" was not always of particular importance, and while such differentiation was widespread in the medieval period, it seemed to fall by the wayside in later years, only resurfacing in the 19th century.

Nowadays, shoe manufacture is an automated process. Until the 19th century when the shoe industry began to develop, however, shoes were largely made on a bespoke basis. Right into the modern period, for example, it was standard practice for people in the country to make their own shoes, while towns had dedicated craftsmen. To be able to make your own shoes was a sign of autonomy and a simple, modest life. Designing and making your own shoes would no doubt have been the best way of stamping your personality on your footwear, followed closely by commissioning a specialist to make shoes to your own specifications.

The Viennese shoemaker Franz Baron offers shoes in both bespoke and regular sizes. Each individual item is created by hand in his workshop.

Mold and Last

"Cobbler, stick to your last"—this proverb is very well known and so we assume that everyone understands what it means. But there are plenty of people who do not know what a "last" is or indeed what a cobbler might do with one. The last is the mold in the shape of a foot on which a shoe is "built."

Since a shoe has to fit a human foot, a last has to have a similar shape, but it is not simply an exact reproduction—even a last for a made-to-measure shoe is more generous in width or height at certain points in order to give the foot ample space, for example at the toes. A separate last for left and right feet has

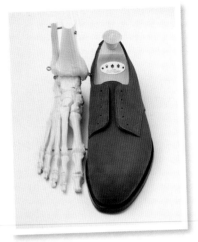

shape known as a "Greek foot" is where the second toe is longer than the big toe, while the longest toe on an "Egyptian foot" is the big toe, with the remaining toes descending in order of size to the little toe. On a "Roman foot," the big toe and the second toe are the same length. The different foot shapes obviously need to be considered when trying on shoes. Health shoes, known colloquially as "duck feet" in their most common form, are not a good fit for Greek feet, for example, as the second toe always knocks against the front of the shoe.

not always been used, however, and for many centuries both shoes in a pair were identical.

Lasts are traditionally made from wood, but industrially manufactured lasts are made of plastic. The shape of the last is determined by the shoe size system and the type of shoe to be made from the last. Generic sized lasts are individually made for each foot, while bespoke lasts are designed to be the closest-matching in shape for a particular foot. Lasts are carved by hand by a craftsman, although since mechanization in 1821, many have also been constructed on a lathe.

Whether, and how well, an off-the-shelf shoe fits an individual's foot is also determined by the shape of the foot; feet can be wide or narrow, and also have insteps of differing sizes. The outer contours of the toes must also be accommodated, and here there are the three common foot shapes to consider. The foot

(Above left) The skeleton reveals whether the shoe fits. The lasts at Eduard Meier make sure that the big toe is not squashed in.
(Below) The foot-measuring gauge at Eduard Meier's shoe store.

The Shoe Size System

Looking for a car is a comparatively easy exercise in terms of choice—you can choose between three, four, or five doors, anything from three to twelve cylinders, and automatic or stick-shift gears.

Buying shoes is a little more difficult, however—while sizes exist, they are not a terribly reliable point of reference. The number inscribed inside a shoe can refer either to the length of the foot or the length of the shoe, so it's hard to tell if the amount of extra space added by the manufacturer to stop the toes jamming against the end of the toecap is included in the size. Also, the different countries that manufacture shoes often use different systems of sizing; this is a result of various factors, such as the British and the Americans use of imperial measurements, for example. The upshot is that when buying shoes you always need to try them on.

Only when you know which size you need from a particular manufacturer can you buy shoes without a fitting—and even then, the size only refers to a particular last, so a different style of shoe might still not fit your feet correctly. In addition, mass-market shoe manufacturers unfortunately only size shoes by length (completely neglecting the width of the foot) and only health shoes and comfort shoes offer two widths at a price that is, on average, still affordable. The shape of the foot is also ignored; most shoes are designed for feet where the big toe is the longest and other toe configurations are not taken into account.

The concept of manufacturing shoes in great numbers, and therefore cost-effectively, is not a new one. One of the reasons it started was that the standing armies maintained in the 18th century

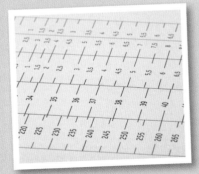

International Sizes

The term "shoe size" suggests that the specific size refers to the dimensions of the shoe; this is not necessarily the case—it is just as likely to refer to the dimensions of the foot. Shoe sizes therefore indicate either the length (and possibly

Only a few manufacturers offer shoes in several width fittings. A very few, such as Eduard Meier in Munich, always have four different widths in store.

had to wear the same uniform, so standardized shoe sizes meant that shoes could be produced for soldiers in workshops that can be considered the forerunners of modern factories. In addition, craftsmen made use of preexisting lasts and quiet periods in the workshop to make shoes to be sold later. Despite all the disadvantages of mass-produced shoes, they must still be considered great progress—even by the early 19th century, the poorer sections of society could afford new shoes only very rarely. Children were obliged to run around barefoot or wore just the most rudimentary footwear. Secondhand, poorly fitting shoes were often the only realistic alternative. These days, most people in the Western world can usually afford to buy shoes. Despite the enormous choice, however, shoe culture is not in the very best of health; even those who can afford good shoes often wear cheap pairs that fail to please the eye and don't do their feet any favors either.

also the width) of the foot or the inside length of the shoe.

The numbers used to indicate the size of shoes are a result of the unit used; British and American shoe sizes are measured in inches, Continental European sizes in millimeters. The gradation between the sizes in Continental Europe amounts to a so-called "Paris stitch": this is a unit 6.66 mm in length, i.e. 2/3 of a centimeter. British and American shoes are gradated in barleycorns, which are measurements of about 1/3 inch, and half-sizes are common here.

There is also the mondopoint system, which is divided into size increments of 5 mm. Despite its precision and ease of use, only the military and safety shoe manufacturers have adopted this system widely.

Leather: Leatherworking and Selection

Leather has been used by humans for thousands of years. It was the material of choice for a great variety of functional and religious objects as well as for decoration; however, it is most closely associated with shoes. As a rule, leather refers to rawhide that has been preserved and strengthened by tanning. It is distinct from fur or pelts, for which the hair of the animal is retained.

Leather was originally a by-product of meat production, but to describe it as a "waste product" would give a false impression of both its value and of our attitude to animals as valuable providers

The American Horween tannery provides the world's best equine leather for shoes.

of sustenance and raw material. In principle, any animal skin can be worked into leather. It is generally produced from cows, pigs, sheep, and also sometimes horses. Cow and calf leather is most often used for top-quality shoes. Because of the high consumption of beef, large amounts are produced, but meat shortages, such as occurred at the end of the 20th century after the cremation of vast numbers of animals due to BSE, result in price hikes for leather.

Leather is produced in several stages. First, the skins are prepared and the hair and subcutaneous fat is removed. The actual tanning process can then begin, and leather is either vegetable- or mineral-tanned. Vegetable tanning involves tanning agents obtained from tree barks, such as oaks or firs, whereas mineral tanning uses a range of natural or synthetic salts. The type of tanning influences the color of the finished product, although natural or synthetic substances can later be used to stain the leather. Fats can also be added to give the leather particular properties.

Lizard leather and snakeskin are considered exotic and are well suited to making shoes.

The Most Important

Suede is one of the napped leathers; these are leathers where the underside of the skin is used or the leather is roughened.

Patent leather is created by adding a coating to what is usually high-quality leather, from cattle or goats, for example.

Woven leather breathes especially well and is thus very popular for summer shoes or sandals. Sourced from a range of animals.

Kinds of Leather

Calf leather or box calf leather (patterned calf leather in the image) is taken from very young calves and used for high-end shoes.

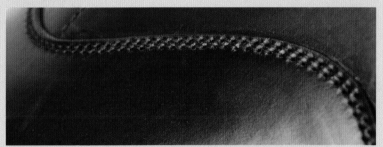

Equine leather (cordovan leather) was once not considered especially desirable and was good value; it is now extremely upmarket.

Reptile leather, such as that obtained from lizards or snakes (crocodile leather in the image) is soft and tough.

Manufacturing Styles

Shoes are made by several different manufacturing styles. However, despite the enormous variety of shoes available, there are far fewer styles of manufacture. The essence of the style lies in the way the sole and the upper are connected. The heel is then attached to the sole.

Blake

MOCCASIN
To make moccasins (and also opankas), the leather upper part is wrapped around the foot from below and originally also formed the outer sole and inner sole. Modern moccasins, such as deck shoes or penny loafers, are generally equipped with an additional inner sole and sometimes a heel.

BLAKE
In the Blake style, the upper and the inner and outer soles are stitched together with a single seam. To prevent water penetrating through the stitching holes, an extra outer sole of leather or plastic is often stuck on. Blake shoes are generally recognizable because of the seams visible on the inner sole, although these are often hidden by an additional thin inner sole.

FLEXIBLE
Flexibly stitched shoes have an upper that is curved out and then sewn to the sole. Flexibly stitched shoes are cheap to produce and generally pretty soft, but do not have much grip.

WELTED
In welted shoes, the upper and the inner sole are connected by a seam to a welt (a strip of leather, plastic, or rubber). The outer sole is then stitched to the welt. The advantage is that the sole can be replaced relatively easily. Welted shoes are somewhat more waterproof than Blake shoes, although water can seep in past the welt.

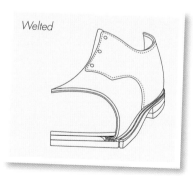
Welted

DOUBLE-STITCHING

Double-stitched shoes are similar to welted shoes and equally complicated to manufacture. Here, the welt is placed outside, against the upper, and then stitched to the inner sole. The outer sole is then stitched to the welt. Mountain boots and hiking boots are generally double-stitched, but it is also traditional in Hungarian shoe-making to use the technique for ordinary street shoes.

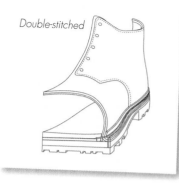

Double-stitched

VELDTSCHOEN

The so-called "Veldtschoen method" is used for manufacturing ordinary hiking shoes and hunting boots. It constitutes the British approach to the double-stitched technique used in Continental Europe and is a variation on the welted method. The lining and the inner sole are connected to the welt via the welt seam. The upper leather section is left untouched before being bent over and stitched to the outer surface of the welt from above. This leaves the shoe largely waterproof.

AGO METHOD

In the early 20th century, the shoe industry was keen to develop cheaper manufacturing methods. The AGO method involves sticking the upper and the outer sole together, a technique that is used for the vast majority of delicate women's shoes and for many cheap men's shoes. Where it is used for top-quality footwear, it is because good shoes have to have finesse and elegance, such as patent leather shoes for evening wear. Shoes with vulcanized or injected soles are even cheaper. Vulcanization is a process for attaching rubber soles and uppers together using heat, while injection molding— a method often used nowadays for mass-produced shoes—involves pouring the plastic sole directly into a mold beneath the upper.

All the various manufacturing methods have their advantages and disadvantages and, of course, a price; the most expensive option is generally considered to be the welted method. (Illustrations: Shoepassion)

Veldtschoen

Double-stitched:

The Haferlschuh, like this one by Meindl,
is worn on a variety of occasions in South
Germany. In black, with a leather sole, it is
also appropriate for more formal occasions.

Handmade, double-stitched shoes are rarely
seen nowadays. Heinrich Dinkelacker's
Hungarian workshop uses this method for
classic half-shoes, which can be fitted with
a molded sole and are certainly suitable for
short walking tours

The light suede model by German manufacturer
Meindl looks particularly summery.

The double-stitching method is particularly
suited to heavy boots as it is both flexible and
hard-wearing. This fashionable example is
also by Meindl.

from Coarse to Fine

A light boot with an adjustable-width upper by the traditional German manufacturer HANWAG, outdoor specialists who have been double-stitching since 1921.

Today, mountain boots are often made with an injected sole. The traditional double-stitched variety is now only available from a few manufacturers, including HANWAG.

Double-stitched leather mountain boots require more care but you will have a shoe that can provide many years of good service. As a natural material, leather still provides the best environment for your feet.

With its genuine lambswool lining, removable thermal inner sole, and adjustable strapping, the HANWAG boot is ideal for general winter use; the tread on the sole also ensures you will not slip.

Sole Varieties

Dainite

The epitome of British rubber soles, Dainite has been manufacturing in Market Harborough since 1894. The Dainite Studded Sole design with its special tread, invisible from the side, was first manufactured in 1910 and is still in use today.

Vibram

The Italian firm Vibram has been making rubber and plastic soles since 1937. They were originally invented to give climbing shoes better grip, but now Vibram soles are available for all kinds of shoes.

Leather

Leather is the traditional material for the outer sole; it can breathe, but is not waterproof over long periods and can slip in the wet. Expensive leather soles are made from vegetable-tanned leather.

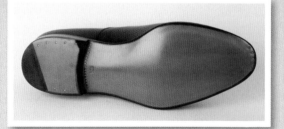

Crepe

Unlike leather soles, crepe soles made from natural rubber are waterproof, although they are difficult to shape, relatively thick, and not resistant to oil or other substances. Crepe also changes shape according to the ambient temperature.

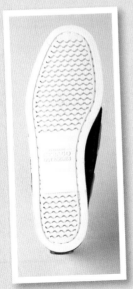

Rubber

Rubber soles have been used to make shoes waterproof and nonslip since the 19th century. Natural rubber soles are now only found on top-quality shoes.

Plastic

For sports shoes and cheap streetwear, the shoe industry now uses soles made from various kinds of plastic, such as polyurethane. The sole and heel are often of one piece and are injected directly onto the shoe.

Studded Sole

The studs on this moccasin, which are visible from the side, are intended to give better purchase on the pedals when driving a car. They are now often found on casual shoes.

Questions

QUESTION: Is there a good substitute material for leather for vegetarians who wish to avoid buying leather shoes?

ANSWER: Lots of people who refuse to eat meat also wear leather shoes without a second thought, while others avoid leather and fur. If vegetarians wish to wear uppers made from natural materials (excluding leather), they are limited to styles in natural fibers such as cotton. Boots from natural rubber or felt would be an option in wet or cold weather. If leather-look shoes are required, styles with a range of synthetic materials could be tried, such as microfiber. The website maintained by the British Vegetarian Shoes brand suggests that their founder uses a kind of synthetic leather that is used for yacht cushions.

QUESTION: Just how environmentally friendly can shoes be?

ANSWER: Lots of shoes claim to be environmentally friendly, and in principle any shoe made of renewable resources is essentially "sustainable," such as a welted shoe with a leather sole and heel—if it is then stitched with hemp twine, it is completely environmentally friendly in terms of the renewability of its materials. Strictly speaking, you should also check how the

animals were fed and whether their feed was organic. If other criteria are also applied, such as the transportation of the raw materials and the finished product, things become more difficult. A truly environmentally friendly shoe is one made by an organic farmer of leather from his own organically raised animals, or a shoe made by a craftsman local to the farmer. The more you think about it, the more doubtful it seems that many of these so-called environmentally friendly shoes are justified in their claims.

QUESTION: There is much talk in the media about carcinogenic substances in shoes. Should I be worried?

ANSWER: Even a doctor or a chemist would find it difficult to answer this question definitively. It would be extremely hard to establish a connection between cancer and the shoes someone has worn before the disease occurred. One would presume it is nonetheless advisable to avoid direct, intensive, and long-term contact between feet and shoes; in other words, always wear socks. While harmful substances can always penetrate through socks to the skin and from the skin into the body, socks do provide a certain amount of protection. As for any connection between skin cancer and shoes, it is worth

& Answers

noting that many people do not look after the skin on their feet properly, not least because feet are usually hidden in shoes. This means that any malignant changes that may occur to the skin in this area are often noticed later than they would be in other areas of the body.

QUESTION: Why do we still use leather for shoes when there are so many good synthetic materials on the market nowadays?

ANSWER: It is not easy to reproduce the beneficial properties of leather—in fact it is almost impossible. Leather can breathe; it is stable, elastic, and hard-wearing; it stores moisture and releases it quickly. It is also sustainable. Man-made, functional materials are usually made from hydrocarbons. Synthetic materials are definitely recommended for specific areas of use, such as plastic soles as shock absorbers or for special boots, but for everyday use, leather has always been best. Unfortunately, only very low-quality leather or even leatherette, made from ground-up bits of leather, is often used for cheaper shoes, so you should always take care to find out what the shoe is made of when making a purchase. This also applies to the inner sole and the lining.

QUESTION: Is it possible that you sweat more in leather shoes with plastic soles? I always find all-leather shoes are the most comfortable.

ANSWER: A shoe made completely of leather can definitely breathe best. That said, a shoe "breathes" through the upper as well, so the plastic sole only has a partial effect. If a shoe is allowed enough time between uses, the sole should not be an issue. Nevertheless, it doesn't matter how good a shoe is if you wear socks made from synthetic fibers—socks made of wool, cotton, linen, flax, or silk are much better. A small amount of elastane in the mix is fine, however.

Brands and Manufacturers

In the world of shoes, much is made of the brand, and a brand is unimaginable without its manufacturer. Having said that, any preconceptions harbored by the average customer about the manufacturer of a brand are often at odds with the reality; the brand's country of origin generally bears little relation to where the shoes are made, and the name representing a brand may have just as little to do with who actually owns the company. Apart from those few individual companies that produce their own shoes or have them made, the brand, its home country, and the place of manufacture are generally only tangentially or not at all related.

A name that sounds Italian, English, or German very rarely represents shoes manufactured in Italy, the UK, or Germany. The description "made in Europe," despite its vagueness, is actually rather valuable. Nowadays, shoes are designed in country A, produced in country B, and then sold in countries A to Z. Only rarely are the design and the production carried out in the same country, as is the case with traditional British shoe brands from Northampton, established welted shoemakers from the USA, or the German health shoe, Birkenstock.

It should be noted that this is not necessarily a criticism; the raw materials for shoes are gathered from a range of countries in any case, and why shouldn't design and production be arranged internationally? When buying a pair of shoes, consumers may believe they are ensuring jobs in their home country, so they just need to be aware that this may not be the case. Criticism of the round-the-world trip made by our shoes can be justified for a number of reasons, however, and it would be misleading to suggest otherwise. It is a question of providing the majority with affordable shoes, and it is easy for those who can afford top-quality "made in Europe" shoes or even handmade shoes from a local craftsman to turn up their noses at cheap shoes from China. Nevertheless, it would be desirable from a consumer point of view for the country of origin to be displayed everywhere, exactly as is prescribed in the USA.

Nowadays, the various shoe models are produced by factories across a range of countries. The greatest variety of welted shoes still comes from the UK (Photo: Cove & Co).

The Most Important Styles

Name: Oxfords. Colors/upper material: black or brown calfskin, less commonly equine leather (cordovan). Suede leather only in brown. History/origins: the Oxford developed from the lace-up or slip-on boot in 19th-century England. Style: the most formal shoe to wear with a suit. When to wear: business, special occasions. Notes: Black Oxfords are worn with morning dress. They can replace a dress shoe in the evenings (must be highly polished). Satin ribbons can be used to good effect as laces.

Name: Oxfords in patent leather. Colors/upper material: black patent leather. History/origins: the evening version of the most formal day shoe. Also known as an Oxford when without a toecap. Style: elegant in the evening. When to wear: only worn with a dinner suit (never with a black day suit). Notes: Normal laces can be replaced with satin ribbons. Never worn during the day.

Name: Monk strap (shortened to "Monk"), buckled shoe. Colors/upper material: black and shades of brown, all kinds of smooth and suede leather. History/origins: the shoe is said to originate from monks' sandals, but it has been known in its current form since the early 20th century. Style: classic, but not conservative, generally too informal for evening wear. When to wear: business (in black) or smart-casual. Notes: The buckle can be matched to your belt buckle. Can also be worn with morning dress, e.g. at weddings or christenings.

Name: Brogue is the original British term; also known as a Budapest shoe, although the latter differs from the brogue in the shape of the last. Colors/upper material: black or brown calfskin or cordovan, or brown suede leather. History/origins: shoes with this Scottish pattern of holes first became fashionable as women's shoes in the 19th century before establishing themselves as sporty men's half-shoes in the 20th century. Style: formal classic. When to wear: in brown, English country look; in black, business. Notes: With its decorative perforations, the black brogue is not suitable for formal evening wear, and its doubled leather sole looks too coarse with a black suit.

The Most Important

Name: loafer, casual, slip-on. Colors/upper material: black and every shade of brown, all kinds of smooth and suede leather. History/origins: slip-on shoes have been around for a while in the form of the pump. In the 20th century these were initially only evening or house shoes, but they have been acceptable as daywear with a suit since the 1930s. Style: sporty to elegant. When to wear: business suit, smart-casual, and leisure. Notes: The smooth black slip-on with a dark suit is also considered too casual in conservative circles.

Name: tasseled loafer. The tassels are decorative ends to the leather laces. Colors/upper material: black and every shade of brown, all kinds of smooth and suede leather. History/origins: invented in the USA in the 1940s and still considered a business classic for bankers and stock-brokers. Style: difficult to slot in between formal and casual wear. Considered a bit déclassé or even tasteless in Europe. When to wear: in black, as a business shoe; in brown, perfect for the smart weekend look. Notes: The tasseled loafer is often compared to the boating blazer, which is neither quite at home as business or leisurewear.

Styles

Name: Derby or Blucher (after the Prussian Marshall Blücher and the boots worn by his troops). Colors/upper material: brown and black calfskin or cordovan. Suede leather only in shades of brown. History/origins: because of its open lacing, the Derby looks sporty, hence the name. Style: a slightly more sporty lace-up. When to wear: depending on color and style, business and formal occasions or smart-casual (in brown, also with a rubber or plastic sole). Recommended for high insteps. Notes: The laces should be crossed.

Name: Oxford loafer, slip-on Oxford. Colors/upper material: black and every shade of brown in suede or smooth leather. History/origins: there is a clear kinship with the ultra-English Oxford and brogue; presumably developed in the 1920s in the wake of the Chelsea boot. The principal feature of this style is the elastic inset on the sides, which makes it easier to get on and also holds the sides sufficiently firmly against the foot. The lack of laces is not noticeable under flared pants, but short or narrow pant legs make the shoe look like a boot when standing. When to wear: as for Oxfords or brogues, in black or brown.

The Most Important Styles

Name: velvet slipper, dress shoe. Colors/upper material: velvet in a range of colors, e.g. red, bottle green, black, violet, or blue with embroidered initials or motif (e.g. animal heads, coats of arms). History/origins: a close relative of the pump, developing to match the velvet smoking jacket as an evening shoe to be worn indoors. Style: English eccentric. When to wear: domestic black-tie events, with a velvet jacket for smokers, with a velvet suit for evening wear.

Name: court shoes, pumps, dress pumps. Colors/upper material: black calfskin with or without a silk or patent leather bow. History/origins: the shoe style that has remained unchanged in a gentleman's wardrobe for the longest period, since the 16th century. Style: genteel, classic. When to wear: definitely required for evening dress, can also be worn with a dinner suit. Only worn during the day for ceremonial or court occasions. Notes: Water-polished calfskin pumps are for many connoisseurs the more genteel alternative to patent leather pumps.

Name: chukka boot. Colors/upper material: a genuine chukka boot is made from brown suede leather as it is a sports shoe. In smooth, black leather it can be used for business, but then tends more toward a laced boot. History/origins: leisurewear for English polo players. Typical of the London Sloane Ranger look. Style: a shoe like an English 4x4, perfect with tweeds, cords, and a waxed jacket. When to wear: country look, ` leisurewear. Notes: Italians wear them with gray or blue brushed flannel.

Name: deck shoe. Colors/upper material: brown, dark blue, white, or in white/brown or white/ blue combinations. History/origins: developed for sailors from the moccasin. Style: sporty, preppy. When to wear: smart-casual and casual. The gentleman's leisure shoe. Notes: Deck shoes can be worn without socks during the summer, although socks are always correct.

Name: sneaker, trainer, gym shoe. Colors/upper material: leather, fabric, synthetic material. History/origins: the sneaker harks back to the simple canvas shoe with a rubber sole that was used in the 19th century for croquet, tennis, and other types of sport. Always popular as a shoe for children, closely related to actual sports shoes. Style: fashionable, trendy, sporty, casual. When to wear: streetwear, leisurewear, fashionable looks. Notes: Sneakers are taboo with business suits and are considered déclassé at formal occasions.

The Great Classics

BASS WEEJUNS

A manufacturer may be justifiably proud if it makes a product that is considered the perfect example of its kind. Burberry managed it with their trench coat and G.H. Bass & Co. have achieved the same with their penny loafer, known as the Weejun. There are of course other good suppliers of this kind of shoe, but the Weejun has established itself as the epitome of the penny loafer. The "penny" part of the name refers to the way college students would adorn their moccasins with a penny placed under the top strap, supposedly to bring good luck, or perhaps just for decoration. The penny loafer by Bass is considered the typical preppy shoe and when yuppie fashion made it to Europe in the 1980s, the Weejun tagged along. The latest preppy revival has brought it to the attention of young fashion fans again.

SPERRY TOPSIDER

There are plenty of deck shoes, but none is as famous as the Sperry Topsider. Fame is always relative and there are many who are unaware of the legendary status still enjoyed by this brand—at least among insiders and connoisseurs—in the USA, the country where this kind of shoe was first worn. The brand's renown rests on the claim that Paul Sperry invented the deck shoe in 1935, supposedly by drawing inspiration from the paws of his terrier to make the nonslip sole. He is said

to have carved grooves in the sole prototype and thus invented a shoe that does not slip on a deck. The Sperry Topsider shoe has become a symbol of preppy lifestyle—sea, beach, and sailing. It soon also became popular with people who could only dream of such a lifestyle.

TOD'S LOAFER

It's a great story—a young man inherits a shoe factory and discovers among the patterns a driving shoe from the 1950s, a soft moccasin with a rubber sole made of small bumps. The sole continues up the heel so that you will not slip when accelerating or changing gear. In addition, the sole protects the heel with a heel cap. The young man was called Diego Della Valle, he named

the loafer "Tod's" and he was something of a PR genius. Legend has it that he sent the shoe to various celebrities so that it would be snapped by paparazzi. The trick worked and the shoes became the casual chic classics of the late 1990s.

SIOUX GRASSHOPPER

Germany is not necessarily considered a fashionable country, but German designs for clothing and shoes have enjoyed global success and have sometimes even set the pace for fashion—we must not forget adidas and PUMA football boots or Brütting running shoes, not to mention Birkenstock health shoes and sandals or Sioux moccasins. Founded in 1954, and bearing a registered trademark since 1956, the Sioux firm produces leisure shoes and streetwear inspired by the footwear worn by Native Americans. The Grasshopper came along in 1964 and 10 million pairs have been sold. It is a soft moccasin with crepe soles and laces, and it fits a range of foot shapes. Clarks obtained the license for the shoe in 1970 and is still selling it today as its classic

Wallabee. Anyone who was a child in the 1960s or 1970s will know the Grasshopper; it was the standard shoe for boys, girls, and teenagers. No one then could have believed that the Grasshopper would still be cool today.

CLARKS DESERT BOOT

Clarks is one of the largest shoe manufacturers in the world and is considered the epitome of all things British. The shoes are no longer made in the UK, admittedly, but this changes nothing about the brand's image and its most famous style, the desert boot. Designed in 1949 and available on the market since 1950, it was Britain's first casual shoe. It works with a range of styles, going just as well with a duffle coat as a tweed jacket, and can be worn by a mod or a grunge fan, a student or a professor. Anyone used to welted shoes and welted versions of the desert boot will not be satisfied with the Clarks original, however—the flexibly sewn design has little grip and the inner sole is of low quality. There is no denying their style, however.

TASSELED LOAFER

The Alden Shoe Company is one of the few remaining manufacturers of high-quality classic men's shoes. There are of

The Clarks desert boot is a typically British classic and looks good with either jeans or a suit.

The original and best tasseled loafer by Alden: the model for numerous slip-on styles of later years.

course other excellent providers of welted shoes in other styles, but Alden leads the field in lace-ups and slip-ons of the highest quality. Very few people will be aware that this company lays claim to the invention of the tasseled loafer, having made one at the behest of a customer in 1948. The shoe, with its decorative tassel, is not uniformly popular, even with connoisseurs, but it is an undisputed classic of men's shoe fashion, comparable with the boating blazer in its positioning midway between formal and casual. In the USA, the tasseled loafer is also considered conservative and can be worn with a dark business suit.

PARABOOT

This Norwegian lace-up by a French manufacturer became one of the most popular casual shoes of top-quality sportswear in the 1980s. A padded moccasin silhouette with a double-stitched plastic molded sole, it goes well with a duffle coat, quilted waistcoat, or Barbour jacket, not to

mention chinos, corduroys, pullovers, or tweed sport coats. The style blends sportiness with a certain elegance, but an elegance unlike the kind normally associated with the British, Americans, or Italians. In any case, this shoe by Paraboot lends the wearer the aura of a smart student who is equally comfortable in a philosophy class as he is in the most expensive fashion boutiques.

GUCCI LOAFER

The name Gucci has stood for expensive designer fashion for decades, but it has sometimes been forgotten that Gucci was originally a leather-maker and the reputation of the company was built on its bags and accessories. Everything else came later, such as the legendary slip-on with the snaffle bit that became the epitome of jet-set style in the 1960s. Fred Astaire wore them, as did English aristocrats and Greek shipping magnates. The loafer was hyped out of all proportion in the 1990s and was available in a range of garish colors before disappearing for a while; it is now a fixed part of the collection again.

DR. MARTENS

German innovation is at the heart of another classic shoe that is generally considered uniquely British: Dr Martens airsole boots. The manufacturer behind them is indeed based in the UK but production is now carried out in Asia. The patent for this successful sole was developed after the Second World War by Klaus Märtens, a German doctor. He began production in Germany with his partner, a native of Luxembourg named Herbert Funck, but in 1960 the British manufacturer R. Griggs & Co. became aware of the German patent for the sole through the specialist press and obtained a license for it. The British designed a new product line and marketed it successfully as a work shoe. Dr. Martens boots have been worn by a range of youth fashion subcultures since the 1960s, and have been recently rediscovered by mainstream fashion as well.

PATRICK COX WANNABE

Patrick Cox, a shoe designer who was born and grew up in Canada, designed a 1990s classic with his Wannabe moccasin. The unisex model was a reinterpretation of the college shoe, although more like its 1970s incarnation. Comfortable and so modern that it was out of the question for fans of classic shoes, the Wannabe was more for fashion victims. It was nonetheless a financially sound idea to get young people interested in something other than sneakers. Much like the Tod's loafer, the Wannabe model was available in a range of different leathers and heel shapes, but the basic design was unmistakable. This made it easy to copy, however, which diluted the brand's reputation somewhat.

BOOT MALTON 1 BY TRICKER'S

When you think of the great shoe classics, you include brogues, Oxfords, and the other timeless standards, of course, but in this section of the book, the "classics" are those styles that represent a particular manufacturer—whose brogue is the epitome of the brogue, for example? In the case of English country boots, you immediately think of Tricker's collections, even if other manufacturers have similar shoes in their range. Tricker's country boots suit Prince Charles just as well as they do a Japanese fashion victim, and between these two extremes, in terms of clientele, you will find all the other fans of these no-nonsense boots from Northampton. Originally developed for hunting and other rural activities, nowadays you are just as likely to find them on a city sidewalk.

The Malton by Tricker's was developed for use in the country, but is also a great favorite of designers.

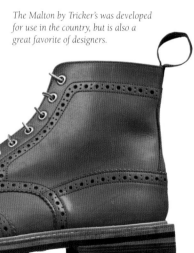

Designer Shoes

The term "designer shoe" is just as misleading as the overall category of "designer fashion"; dedicated shoe designers have been in existence ever since the industrial manufacture of shoes began. While they may originally have been called shapers, makers, or modelers, their task was identical to that of their modern counterparts. Where we talk about designer shoes in this book, however, for the most part we mean shoes by famous designers and/or by designers who have devoted themselves to designing shoes—although there are exceptions, of course.

When you think of designer shoes or shoe designers, you immediately think of women's shoes, and here we could mention famous names like Salvatore Ferragamo, Jimmy Choo, or Christian Louboutin. The simple reason for this is that women's fashion has been promoting constant change as a prerequisite for elegance for much longer than men's fashion has, which is why it is absolutely critical that designers of women's fashion continually deliver new and sensational creations. On the other hand, men have preferred continuity in their fashion over the decades, and radical change has not been on the agenda. However, designers, or at least brands, have grown in importance for men since the 1980s; under the leadership of well-known designers, fashion brands are gaining in prestige and becoming desirable for many consumers.

As astronomical prices are often charged for designer shoes, with no commensurable value on offer, the term "designer shoe" has come to have a negative resonance for many people, but this does not alter the appeal designer shoes have for those who buy the brands, of course.

The fashion designer John Varvatos has brought out his own collection for Converse, reinterpreting the sneaker manufacturer's classics in new and surprising ways.

Designer shoes don't always have to look classy and luxurious—John Varvatos sometimes goes for the "used look" for Converse.

Chucks with a zip by John Varvatos—design sometimes means altering the familiar beyond all recognition and opening up new perspectives.

Paul Falke
on Shoes

....

" Like socks, shoes are an important and

essential accessory; they round off an outfit

and make a fashion statement. In choosing my

shoes I set great store by perfect craftsmanship

and the best quality. Handmade welted shoes

by Heschung, Alden, Santoni, or Dieter

Kuckelkorn possess all these qualities. The

styles I prefer are classics such as the Monk,

the cap toe Derby, or also Chelsea boots. "

....

*The fabric merchant Paul Falke is an Epicurean, an aesthete, and a fanatic
about quality, which is why the headquarters of the Falke Group in the Sauerland
in Germany has a workshop in which the best socks are made by hand. Falke has
been a byword for courageous fashion for years, always looking for fresh colors
and designs in his collections.*

Types of Shoe Store

Until the beginning of the industrial revolution, shoes in Europe were largely made by small-scale craftsmen. In times of unemployment or low demand, they would often make some pairs in advance, ready for when business picked up. When the shoe industry increased its output, many of these small-time craftsmen were taken on as retailers, creating small shoe stores that even today still make shoes to measure, as well as providing a repair service and selling finished goods.

Some enterprising shoe manufacturers have always sold their products in their own shops, while nowadays department stores also provide customers with a selection of shoes.

DEPARTMENT STORES

The quality and breadth of range of the shoe sections in international department stores are dependent on a number of factors and also take into account cultural considerations. In France and Spain, for example, it would be perfectly normal to buy exclusive fashion in a suitably upmarket department store, whereas in Germany this would be unusual.

If the selection of shoes and the advice provided is good, there can be no objections to buying shoes in a department store, of course (assuming, that is, that you need or would like advice). And if you know exactly what you want, you may make a find when hunting for bargains.

SHOE CHAINS

There are plenty of chain stores and the range of shoes provided covers everything from cheap, low-quality footwear to welted masterpieces. It simply depends on what you are looking for and how much you can or would like to spend. High-quality shoe chains often have their own brand, offering better value for money than their famous-name competitors and occasionally even entry-level welted shoes.

LARGE, INDEPENDENT SHOE STORES

There are generally fewer traditional large specialist shops internationally today, but there is still a good selection of well-stocked establishments that are run with enthusiasm; these are sometimes located in smaller towns or in the country. As a rule you won't find welted shoes or off-the-wall brands, but there are plenty of exceptions to the rule.

OUTLET CENTERS

Everybody loves a special offer, which is why outlet centers are so popular. However, do make sure that the shoes really are from the brand's regular collection and have not just been manufactured cheaply for this particular sales channel.

FACTORY OUTLETS

Some shoe manufacturers operate small shops right next to the factory premises to sell B-grade wares or other individual pairs at lower prices. As midprice shoes are often made in other countries, genuine "factory shops" are thin on the ground, certainly in European cities, and these are in fact mostly outlet centers.

INDEPENDENT RETAILERS

Small shoe stores have a fight on their hands these days, with fierce competition from discount stores, shoe chains, and the Internet. There have always been niches, however, and these can be filled by resourceful independent stores with an interesting range of shoes.

LUXURY SHOE STORES

The prime locations in large cities are home to shoe stores selling footwear with extremely expensive price tags. These are either the "flagship stores" of shoe labels, or independent companies offering a range of shoes consisting mainly of expensive designer brands.

GENTLEMEN'S OUTFITTERS

Exclusive menswear shops led the field for top-quality shoes in the 1980s, especially as independent shoe shops largely slept through the trend for highly expensive shoes and often lacked sales staff who had the right attitude to sell the product.

SPECIALIST STORES

Selling welted shoes is an art in itself. The product is very expensive and the clientele well-informed and highly mobile. If you want to keep your customers coming, you have to present your wares with competence and charm.

BESPOKE SHOEMAKERS

As a rule, shoes from a bespoke shoemaker are the most expensive. Off-the-shelf shoes are not usually on display, and the store window only features examples of the models that can be produced in-house. The craftsman thus has to initially sell his skills rather than his wares, an art mastered by very few.

Upmarket footwear needs a proper setting such as this: Crockett & Jones in London's Knightsbridge.

Distance Purchasing

In addition to all the usual shoe retailers, nowadays there are more and more discount stores and a range of options on the Internet. Online purchasing isn't an entirely new concept, as shoes have been bought by mail order for a very long time. The main problem with purchasing footwear online is that the shoes cannot be tried on, so the returns policy is crucially important—otherwise it really is only worth buying shoes at a distance when you know how they will fit.

DIRECT SALES

More and more manufacturers are selling their shoes by direct sale. If a manufacturer isn't doing this, it is often because they don't wish to upset independent retailers, who are not always delighted to see their supplier become their competitor.

The Berlin-based Internet shoe store Shoepassion wants to be more than a distance sales outlet; its goal is to provide comprehensive information about the whole subject of shoes on its website.

Buying shoes online has advantages and drawbacks: in the first place, you can't try them on. You also miss out on the whole sensual experience—you can't smell, feel, or see the leather. On the other hand, you have peace of mind and can compare prices directly on the Internet, and as a result more men are now buying shoes online from the comfort of their own home, especially as returns are easy to make.

INTERNET SHOE STORES

Shoes are generally bought on the Internet if the range is good and the returns policy generous; this makes it fun to order several pairs and only keep the ones that really fit, or even to send them all back.

CATALOGS

Shoes have been successfully sold from catalogs since the 19th century. Because of the enormous distances involved, this sales channel has a long tradition in the USA. The Internet now often replaces the printed catalog, but ultimately it is still the same business.

ONLINE AUCTION HOUSES

If you are an expert or have special needs, you should be able to find interesting or suitable shoes at online auctions. The feedback system means that, in general, sellers are both accommodating and friendly.

Tips for Buying Shoes

Why do people buy shoes? It makes a big difference whether you actually need shoes or whether you are buying just for the pleasure of shopping. Choosing shoes according to fashion criteria is a different matter from buying them for fit; if you are buying shoes for fun or fashion, essentially you can make your purchase in any shop you like—the fit is of secondary importance if you are more interested in a trendy look. If you are looking for shoes that fit well, however, or perhaps want them to last a bit longer, try to bear the following few essential points in mind:

1 You should always have your feet measured, even if you think you know your size, and especially if you don't. Your foot size changes over the course of your life and it is easy to find yourself wearing the wrong size shoes for a number of years. Both the length and the width of your feet must be measured, although not that many shoes are available in a variety of widths (or breadths). If you have a particularly narrow or wide foot, you will definitely need a specially shaped shoe, and these are not easy to come by. Only manufacturers of health shoes or top-quality welted shoes offer styles in two (or sometimes more) widths.

2 Always try the shoe on. If you are keen on distance purchasing, be prepared for a particular size not to fit you when buying shoes. It is much better to buy two pairs and then choose which pair fits best, but if they don't fit, don't compromise—it's not a good idea to wear badly fitting shoes.

3 A shoe fits correctly when it firmly encloses the middle of your foot. It shouldn't pinch, of course, but the foot should not be able to slip forward. The toes need enough room at the tip of the shoe, and under no circumstances should they touch the inside of the toecap. You should also be able to move your toes.

4 If you are concerned about avoiding sweaty feet, you should only wear shoes made from natural materials. This applies to the upper, the lining, and the inner sole. Cheap shoes are often made entirely from plastic and the same is true for most sneakers. Adverts might try to suggest that synthetic inner soles can breathe, but leather is always best. All this is no benefit at all, however, if your socks are not made of cotton or wool. Even a small proportion of synthetic fibers can result in sweaty feet and foot odor.

5 You can tell a correct fit not only from the way your toes feel, but from how the shoes sit on your instep. People with high insteps often feel cramped by closed laces (e.g. with an Oxford). Shoes with open lacing, such as a Derby, may fit a high instep better. If you just don't like things pushing down on your instep, you can wear Monks with a double buckle, which will distribute the pressure more evenly. Laced or elasticized boots are also a good alternative. Slip-on shoes are problematical as they hold the instep tightly.

6 Leather is not always leather. To be described as "leather," "genuine leather," or "pure leather," animal skins have to be processed directly with no intervention; scraps of leather that are ground up and then made into a synthetic product using some kind of adhesive are not leather. So-called "top-grain" leather is rather less valuable than the outer skin of the animal and is made by cutting or scraping off the outer skin in several layers. Very thin top-grain leather, which is coated with plastic, must be declared as such and is often used for sneakers.

Bespoke Means the Right Fit

IF YOU BUY BESPOKE, YOU DON'T HAVE TO BOTHER TRYING ON LOTS OF PAIRS OF SHOES.

The bespoke shoe experience begins with measuring the feet, and a variety of methods can be used. In the simplest cases, measurements are taken of foot length and width, but these are often supplemented by outlines of the foot.

Less commonly, the craftsmen will make three-dimensional molds, but this is only really necessary for problematic feet. Experienced last-makers employ an expert eye and the obligatory manual inspection.

Shoe Fans: Hunters

There must be something in what the American author Nicholas Antongiavanni says in his book *The Suit*, where he maintains that a gentleman's suit can be compared with his house, while shoes occupy the same place in his life as his car. The comparison is apt, as footwear is both a way of getting around and an object of desire, passion, and love.

Discussions about shoes, like those about cars, can be quite incomprehensible to outsiders—few know what an "insole lip" is, or why "handstitched" is better than "Goodyear-welted," or where "shell cordovan" comes from. Admittedly, one aspect of the analogy is less appropriate: most men are interested in cars, while shoes are a matter of indifference to the majority of the male population, who see them simply as a practical necessity on which the least amount of money possible should be spent.

For an increasingly small but select minority, however, stylish footwear is an essential prerequisite for quality of life—an expression of culture, a source of secret joy. The members of this cult live beneath the radar of the majority; those who wish to belong need no identity card, just the right shoes, and you must of course also know that "insole lip" does not refer to an unfortunate medical condition but rather to a flap underneath the inner sole to which the leather of the upper is attached by hand ("handstitched")

and Gatherers

or machine ("Goodyear-welted"), and that we have horses to thank for "shell cordovan."

Most shoe enthusiasts will remember the exact moment when their passion began, their "first time." For some it will have been a sudden glance in a store window, for others the pair of shoes given to them by their father for their 18th birthday. Sometimes this shoe enthusiasm will lead even a young man to an extravagant desire for bespoke shoes.

There are, of course, other kinds of shoe passions—collectors of sporty footwear are known as "sneakerheads" and some of these have a matching pair of sports shoe for every T-shirt they own. Others will camp out all night in front of a shop in which a limited edition sneaker will go on sale the next day. It is not uncommon for these same sneakers to be hoarded subsequently for years in a wardrobe and never worn—for a fanatic, it's enough to unpack their treasures from time to time for inspection, not least because pristine, unworn shoes in their original boxes can sometimes be sold for considerable profits in online auctions. There are also rare sneakers whose price can exceed by some considerable margin that of a pair of even the best bespoke shoes.

The bespoke tailors Cove & Co. also considers itself a specialist for welted shoes.

Questions

QUESTION: How healthy are so-called health shoes?

ANSWER: Health shoes generally look pretty unattractive. They are wide, shaped like a duck's foot at the front, and of late have been fitted with a curiously shaped special sole that is supposed to be especially good for the back. Are these shoes as healthy as they are unattractive? Health shoes are certainly designed to be good for feet: manufacturers develop shapes that are intended to support the foot and not cramp the toes, but these shapes are only beneficial if they fit your foot exactly. This is where health shoes suffer from the same problems as other off-the-shelf shoes—they often don't fit. Welted shoes, on the other hand, are healthy for feet and look good too—with the usual proviso that they fit well, with the correct width and length, and in a style that suits the shape of your foot.

QUESTION: With designer shoes, are you actually just paying mainly for the name?

ANSWER: How much the "name" affects the price of a designer shoe varies with the material and manufacturing method. If a simple linen sneaker from a designer's collection is much more expensive than a standard model, you are generally paying for the label. If a designer shoe is welted or otherwise hand-finished, however, look more closely at the materials; sometimes extremely high-quality materials are used for such shoes, and these can then be really expensive.

QUESTION: I have had my size measured exactly in the shoe store. Can I now buy shoes without trying them on in future?

ANSWER: Only people who buy the same model regularly from the same manufacturer, with no change of last, can afford to do so without trying the shoes on—over the short term at least. Otherwise the fit should always be checked. In addition, sizes can vary with the manufacturing process. Moccasins, for example, should be bought in a size or so smaller than lace-ups.

QUESTION: I have narrow feet and can thus rarely find shoes that fit in the stores. Do different nationalities have wider or narrower feet?

ANSWER: Do Americans have wider feet than the British, for example? Do people living in different parts of the same country have different foot widths? Interestingly, Peter Herkenrath, whose shoe store in Cologne, Germany, is crammed full of upmarket brands, confirms this suggestion:

& Answers

"Americans and Brits have narrower feet than the Germans. In Germany, feet get wider, stronger, and fatter from north to south."

In principle, the bespoke shoemaker Benjamin Klemann from Hamburg agrees, but for him, these broad German feet are the result of a deformation: "Splayed feet have spread through the whole of Germany." Is this anecdotal evidence or fact? The traditional firm of Fagus is Germany's market leader in the manufacture of lasts and makes the basic molds for the mass market; who else would have a better idea of German feet? A Fagus spokesman told us: "Over the last 20 years, our lasts have got wider by an average of 5 mm [3/16 inch]."

But what does this prove? Just that people who like to buy German brands like wide shoes. Peter Eduard Meier, the owner of the Eduard Meier shoe store in Munich and an experienced last-maker, maintains: "Most people wear shoes that are too wide, which is why they are always slipping forward in their shoes and their toes are rubbing against the front of the shoe. The result is that they buy bigger shoes. Shoes only fit when they hold the middle of the foot tightly enough that it cannot slip forward."

QUESTION: Where do well-known brands actually get their shoes from?

ANSWER: Someone buying Italian-branded shoes, for example, might well suppose that they were made in Italy. Nowadays, unfortunately, it is often the case that the brand and the shoe do not originate in the same country; an Italian-branded shoe may come from China or Romania, for example, certainly as far as the place of production is concerned. This is not necessarily a problem, of course, but the consumer could still perhaps be disappointed, and may even feel cheated. The example of Italian shoes also applies to German or French labels as well.

The origins of a shoe are easier to ascertain in the USA, where the provenance has to be stated exactly. In the case of top-quality shoes, however, the place of manufacture often has the same location as the company's headquarters: welted footwear by Alden is made at the family firm's base in the USA, just as high-end shoes from established English brands are made in the UK, or Birkenstock's sandals are made in Germany. If someone is not keen on their shoes coming from China, they should consider the price they are prepared to pay for their shoes—anyone wishing to purchase the latest trends every season at knockdown prices should not be surprised to find that they come from a country where workers are paid low wages and that the shoes have been cobbled together from less than top-grade materials.

Welted Shoes

Welted shoes—a phrase with an undeniable magic resonance for connoisseurs. Welted shoes stand for quality, robustness, and classic styling, not to mention cult appeal, shopping addiction, and status; men who wear welted shoes might sometimes even be tempted to look down slightly on those who do not.

Welted shoes have been produced industrially in Europe since the 19th century, with the invention of sewing machines patented by the American Charles Goodyear in 1869 making it possible to speed up work processes that had previously been completed by hand. The parts of the upper have also been stitched together mechanically since the end of the 19th century, even by bespoke shoemakers who tout their products as "handmade." There were manufacturers of these shoes in most European countries until the 1970s, but production has slowly dwindled. Manufacture of these shoes is now concentrated in the USA, England, Spain, and France. Welted shoes are also manufactured in India and Sri Lanka, but these are generally made with cheaper kinds of leather.

As interest in formal clothes waned across the board in the 1960s and 1970s, young people also lost a sense of the value of classic shoes. However, as every trend is inevitably followed by a countertrend, the 1980s saw a revival of top-quality, hand-made clothes—yuppie and Sloane Ranger style, which was then imitated internationally—and top-drawer footwear was required. The look cultivated by well-dressed Italians (and copied throughout the world) set great store by welted shoes from England and brought the shoe back into the spotlight. Any young man who discovered the welted shoe for himself in the 1980s is likely to have remained loyal to it ever since. The children of die-hard shoe fans often catch the same bug and it is not uncommon for them to be given a pair of good shoes by their father, perhaps after graduating from high school or at the latest when starting their first job, as a sign of the first steps into adult life.

Welted shoes are made in such a wide range of styles that every taste in fashion is catered for. This is a buckled shoe from the Saint Crispin's collection.

Handstitched vs the

A person who buys welted shoes is generally more interested in footwear than the average man, but he is not likely to inquire too deeply into the finer points of the materials used in their creation. He assumes that he is getting a "handmade" shoe of the highest quality for his money. The difference between a truly handmade shoe from the workshop of a craftsman and a shoe that comes out of a factory is not one that he is really aware of, and most sales staff are happy not to disabuse him of the notion that shoes from famous brands such as Crockett & Jones, Alden, or Church's are made by hand—or indeed they may actually believe it themselves. Strictly speaking, all of these shoes are made in factories, even though they may be described as "workshops" or "ateliers."

Making a bespoke shoe by hand: the shoemaker sews the welt, leather upper, and inner sole together.

This is neither a drawback nor an attempt to mislead, it should be noted, and sometimes shoes from a factory may even be superior to those from a small workshop. But people should simply know the difference, which is mainly the fact that—in an ideal case—the craftsman really does produce a last by hand and then, later on in the production process, draws the upper over the last by hand, tacks it securely, and then also carries out the sole-making work on the shoe by hand. In a factory, all of this work is done by machines which have been especially designed to save time while achieving the same results. These machines are of course operated by experts; the individual parts of the shoe do not just roll down a conveyor belt to be assembled by machine and tipped out at the other end as completed footwear.

Shoemakers, sales staff, fashion journalists, and shoe experts are often passionately at odds over which shoe is better—one from a factory or one from a craftsman's workshop. Dedicated Internet forums discuss the problem back and forth, with positions defended to the very last stitch, as it were.

Goodyear Method

We should first define exactly what it is that we are comparing. A shoe from a factory which has used only the best quality leather and other components and which has maintained the highest levels of manufacturing standards can only be compared with a handmade shoe produced to a similar high quality. The fact that something has been assembled by hand in a little workshop is not really a statement of its quality. It is, however, a fact that the old, traditional shoe factories, such as those found in Northampton in the UK, have access to much more superior kinds of leather than a small craftsman does, and also that a small craftsman would have to achieve a higher quality with his own hands and his tools than the standard achievable with the help of custom-made machinery. To what extent the fit should be included when assessing the quality of a shoe is also debatable, as it isn't always clear which is preferable: a better fitting bespoke shoe of average-quality manufacture or a

Using a machine in the factory; the Goodyear machine replaces the manual process.

generic-sized factory-made shoe of arguably better quality.

Discussion of the pros and cons of both kinds of welted shoe revolves around a small but important detail on the underside of the inner sole. In factory-made shoes, a narrow strip of leather, known as the rib, is attached to the bottom of the inner sole with adhesive tape, and the upper and the welt are attached to this strip with a single seam. In handmade shoes, no such strip of leather is attached and instead a thicker inner sole is used. This inner sole is then hollowed out from below until the outer edge stands proud. The upper and welt are then stitched to this. Proponents of the factory process see it as an advantage that the strip is glued, as *in extremis* it can be replaced (after several repairs the strip can break). Supporters of the handmade approach argue that the shoe is far more stable when the strip is part and parcel of the inner sole and is not glued on separately.

Factory-made

The listed factory building owned by Crockett & Jones in Northampton in the UK produces welted shoes of extraordinarily high quality. The staff are often the second or third generation of a family to work here.

Welted Shoes

Lasts for every style and size await use. Nowadays they are made of resilient plastic.

The individual parts of the upper are connected using sewing machines. This used to be exclusively women's work.

The lining is stitched to the leather upper, a process which is carried out with a sewing machine; even bespoke shoemakers do not do this by hand.

The outer sole is sanded into shape. The shoe is wrapped in clear film to protect it from scratches.

The outer sole is dyed to match the upper, which both protects it and makes it look good—this is properly "handmade."

Wax paste is rubbed into the upper, which is then polished by hand to give the shoe its provisional color.

Handmade

The owners of the Baden-Baden bespoke shoemaker's Vickermann & Stoya in their workshop in Germany. Although the firm was only founded in 2004, it has already achieved wide renown.

Lasts line the shelves; the name reveals whose feet they are designed to fit.

The sewing machines in the workshop are older than the firm itself.

Welted Shoes

The various tools in the workshop are not there for decorative purposes but are used on a daily basis.

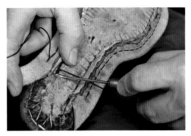

Bespoke shoes are traditionally stitched by hand—this means that the upper, welt, and inner sole are joined together manually.

A layer of cork is applied beneath the inner sole; the foot will make its individual impression on this as the shoe is worn.

The Greatest

USA

At the end of the 19th century a great number of factories were established in the USA to make welted shoes using what was then the new Goodyear method. Only a few of them have survived to the present day, but they continue to deliver the highest quality. In addition, cowboy, work, and hunting boots are still made in the USA using the Goodyear process.

Alden Founded in Massachusetts in 1884 and known in Europe mainly for its cordovan shoes. Comprehensive, classic American collection. Several widths.

Allen Edmonds Welted shoes with round edging and no steel strut. The original advertising claim that these shoes did not need to be worn in still applies.

England

Dozens of shoe manufacturers settled in and around Northampton from the end of the 19th century to the 1960s, although only a relatively small number remain today. This district in England's East Midlands is nonetheless a global center for the manufacture of high-quality welted shoes.

Church's Shoes One of Northampton's most famous names, although its image took a knock after a takeover by Prada in 1999. It is now back on track, although many of its old customers have jumped ship.

Crockett & Jones Supposedly the best manufacturer in England, it has held this reputation for some time now. Available around the world, output is limited by in-house production and highly stringent quality control.

Cheaney A supplier of excellent shoes. Founded in 1886, it still lives somewhat in the shadow of the other big names. One of the few brands to also make shoes in the Veldtschoen style.

John Lobb Part of the Hermès Group since 1976. The brand's factory-made shoes have been manufactured in Northampton since 1994. Bespoke shoes are available from the London headquarters in St. James's Street and in Paris, France.

Edward Green Considered the first among equals of the Northampton shoe factories, it has been making shoes that stand out through the finest craftsmanship and bespoke finish since 1890.

Grenson One of the old family firms, with less of a reputation despite its excellent quality. Has acquired a more modern image of late, while the shoes remain of equally good quality.

Brands ...

Tricker's An established Northampton institution, and famed for its Country Collection, Tricker's is purveyor of shoes to the Prince of Wales. Tricker's shoes are also popular on the fashion scene for their authenticity.

Barker A dependable manufacturer from Northampton, founded in 1880, with a comprehensive, if slightly fusty collection, but solid at heart.

Alfred Sargent This company has been making welted shoes in Northampton since 1899 and has recently stepped out from beneath the shadow of the other more famous brands.

Gaziano & Girling Welted shoes either fully bespoke, made-to-order, or off-the-shelf, with a workshop located in Northampton. Plenty of trunk shows in Europe and the USA.

Benelux

It may come as a surprise to learn that there are actually three manufacturers producing top-quality welted men's shoes in the Netherlands and Belgium, although shoes of this kind are not the principal export of either country.

Netherlands

Greve Greve has been making welted shoes of the highest quality and hand-stitched moccasins in the Noord-Brabant region of the Netherlands since it was founded in 1898.

van Bommel This family firm of welted shoe manufacturers was founded in 1734 and has held a Dutch royal warrant since 1952.

Belgium

Ambiorix This factory has been making shoes by the Goodyear method since its foundation in 1895. Its production output and high levels of quality mean it is still an insider tip.

Germany

Welted shoes have not been made industrially in Germany since the 1970s. The few providers of welted shoes left in the country either produce very small runs or offer bespoke work; their collections are otherwise made in Eastern Europe, Spain, or England. This has had no negative consequences on the quality and so they make no secret of it.

... Around

Heinrich Dinkelacker Specialist in welted and double-stitched shoes, which have been made in their in-house workshop in Budapest since the 1960s.

Dieter Kuckelkorn A native of the spa town of Aachen, who designs his collections in Germany before having them made in very short runs in his Spanish workshop. As Dieter himself admits, the lasts only fit Central European feet.

Eduard Meier A traditional Munich firm with its own collection, developed entirely independently on its own lasts. Factory-made and handstitched welted shoes.

Cavallo Founded in 1978 as a riding-boot maker, Cavallo also offers welted boots for everyday use and welted half-shoes. The majority are made in Germany.

Austria

Austrian and Hungarian shoemakers are still reaping the benefits of the great reputation that their creations enjoyed across Europe until the Second World War. A variety of shoemakers have survived to the present day in Austria and there is also a reasonable number of manufacturers of welted shoes in the country, although some have farmed out production to cheaper neighboring countries.

Alt Wien Welted shoes on typical Austrian lasts with classic styles for every season.

Ludwig Reiter A factory founded in Vienna in 1885 to make welted shoes has now become the largest manufacturer in Austria. Its range includes both classics and modern styles.

Saint Crispin's Handmade welted shoes, both off-the-shelf and made-to-order, made in Romania. The showroom is in Vienna but most sales are made through gentlemen's outfitters.

Hungary

László Vass Traditional, handstitched welted shoes from the resurgent Hungarian shoemaking industry. A comprehensive collection that is available in Budapest and a few other places internationally.

France

With a style that lies somewhere between that of the British and the Italians, French shoe manufacturers win fans and favor with their elegant designs and careful finishing. The British traditionally have a strong position in France's domestic market, but French manufacturers also enjoy an excellent reputation.

the World

Aubercy Founded in 1935, this Parisian workshop has its typically French collection made by Italian artisans.

Berluti Legendary bespoke shoemaker with a factory-made collection. Idiosyncratic shapes and colors make them unmistakable.

Corthay A Parisian shoemaker with a small selection of ready-to-wear handstitched welted shoes with a refined French look.

J. M. Weston Founded in Limoges in 1891, the brand has a great reputation in France. In addition to the shoe factory, the company also owns its own tannery.

Italy

Italy, the land of fashion, has no great tradition of making Goodyear-welted shoes. Factories were more concerned with making light and fashionable footwear after the Second World War, and the Italians tend to prefer the British brands of welted shoes. A few firms have nonetheless made a name for themselves, often providing top-quality manufacturing methods, designs, and finishes.

Silvano Lattanzi Silvano Lattanzi has been making small runs of handstitched welted shoes and bespoke shoes since 1965.

Sutor Mantellassi A small label for first-class luxury men's shoes. The range includes shoes made with all the top-quality manufacturing methods.

Santoni Unusually wide-ranging manufacturer offering all the upmarket manufacturing methods, including the Goodyear welt, handstitched welted shoes, double-stitched, and Blake.

Spain

Spain has a long tradition of leatherworking stretching back to the time of the Moors. Welted shoes have been made since the 19th century and, although the domestic companies remain somewhat in the shadow of their British and American rivals, the last decade has seen them carve out a confident niche for themselves due to their high quality products.

Carmina Founded in Mallorca in 1997, this company is a newcomer by comparison. They make welted shoes using the Goodyear method and sell through their own chain of stores or via independent retailers.

Lotusse Founded on Mallorca in 1877 and now run by the fourth generation of the family. They make welted shoes using the Goodyear method.

Made in France: Corthay in Paris

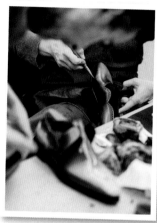

Two seats from a 1964 Fiat Dino that have been converted into a couch lend the small lobby an air of an automobile magnate's waiting room, but this is dispelled by the smell of turpentine wax polish emanating from a glass container in which a young man is just dipping the tip of a cloth he has wrapped around his hand. He moistens the same spot with a little water and, with circular movements, goes to work on the toecap of a brown shoe, which is then dulled by the polish he has just applied. After about a minute of rubbing, a kind of film forms on the silky surface of the leather and over the course of another two minutes transforms itself into a mirror shine. Time is of only secondary importance in the atelier of the Parisian shoemaker Pierre Corthay—they would otherwise not devote the 50 or 60 hours of work required for every single one of the 150 pairs of shoes that are created by the four employees here every year.

The Rue Volney is not far from Place Vendôme in the second *arrondissement* and the atelier on the ground floor of number 1 is reached through an arch. Pierre Corthay takes care of the design and cutting of the upper parts, and his younger brother Christophe makes the lasts. When a client orders a shoe for the first time, both brothers will be in attendance to measure the length, breadth, and dimensions of the feet, and an outline of the feet is also recorded on paper. Working from memory and this data, Christophe will carve the last from a wooden blank, in the cellar underneath the offices. It is not just an exact physical representation of each foot, but also the negative mold of the shoe that will be produced. As the shoe is made of leather, it cannot fit as snugly on the foot as a sock; a shoe has to fit firmly on the heel and instep, so the foot does not slip around, but additional length is required at the tip to allow the toes to move. The last should also have an appropriate and well-proportioned shape, and one that meets the wishes of the client.

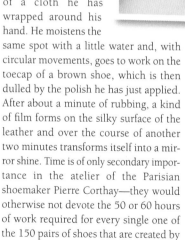

Pierre Corthay draws in the parts of the upper on the finished last with a pencil before transferring the outlines of the leather parts onto supple card from which he cuts the templates for the individual components. The leather is cut by hand too, just as the upper-maker makes each individual "broguing" hole with a hammer and a punch. He then stitches all the individual parts together, adds the lining and pulls the completed upper over the last. The inner sole is temporarily nailed to the underside so that it can be hollowed out to form the welt seam on its outer edge. This is where the upper and the welt will later be stitched together by hand.

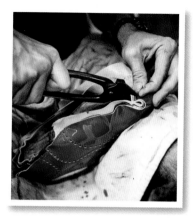

The Corthay workshop in Paris uses ancient shoemaking methods; the shoes that are handmade here, however, are extremely modern and often very chic.

For new customers, a test shoe is first created. If this shoe fits the customer's foot to their satisfaction, the final shoe can be made. The test shoe both demonstrates the constant striving for a perfect fit and is also part of the ritual. Professionals like the Corthays usually get the shoe right first time, but it is just these little nuances between "good" and "perfect" that make all the difference for a bespoke shoe enthusiast. In addition, a certain percentage of their clientele have problematic feet and for these people a satisfactory solution can only be achieved with a trial run.

The speed and confidence with which Pierre Corthay works is the result of comprehensive training and many years of experience. As a wandering apprentice he learned every aspect of the profession for six years before spending 18 months with John Lobb in Paris. He then managed the Berluti workshop for five years before setting up his own business in 1990. In 1996 he recruited Christophe, who had just finished his shoemaker's apprenticeship. Pierre looks youthful, with an unpretentious manner: a mixture of self-confidence and modesty that marks out many craftsmen. He is wearing a purple shirt, no tie, jeans, and—of course—his own shoes.

The staff also don't really fit the image of a shoemaker that press photos seem keen to portray: instead of hunched old men myopically poking an awl through a scrap of leather, the Rue Volney is full of young men wearing jeans with their work apron, just like their boss; except for the fact that they are all sporting exquisite shoes, they could be taken for students. Corthay's styles encompass the classics—Oxford, Derby, brogue, and tasseled loafer—but he tries to give them a new twist with small details or altered proportions.

The Bernay boot, for example, is a mixture of Chelsea boot and chukka boot, while the Rascaille loafer incorporates the typical features of the penny and full-strap loafer in one. The leather store is piled high with skins of every shade— red, blue, orange, green, Bordeaux, purple, and yellow, but the wearers of his creations are not all eccentrics or fops, as Corthay makes clear; they simply possess a strong sense of individuality. The majority are bankers and lawyers, although his clientele also includes art and antiques dealers.

Corthay's range of styles includes the "usual suspects" offered by almost every shoemaker, but also a few specialties that showcase the interplay of colors, patterns, and leather varieties beloved of French master craftsmen. Green and blue are almost standard colors here and workaday brown is enlivened with a mix of materials or a particularly shiny finish. For his evening shoes, classic black patent leather is complemented with yellow gold laces. Shoes like this are not necessarily to the taste of those who prefer the British gentleman look.

Christian Rainer on Shoes

....

"*I saved up for my first pair of bespoke shoes when I was just a student and to this day I mostly prefer to wear handstitched shoes. I think of my style as 'modern dandy' and shoes like that are just a part of it. They have to be properly looked-after as well, I polish my shoes regularly. It is a kind of barometer of how I am feeling. I always say that men stop polishing their shoes just before they are ready to commit suicide. So—watch my feet.*"

....

Austrian journalist Christian Rainer is also a lawyer and an economist, Editor and Editor-in-Chief of the successful economics and news magazine Bergsteiger, a father, a workaholic, and one of the best-dressed men in his home country. Despite his humor, he is entirely serious about what he says.

Bespoke Shoemakers

England

London was once the world center for classic menswear. Unfortunately, standards have somewhat slipped since those halcyon days and much is in flux, with a few of the old, established firms having gone under.

John Lobb The king of shoemakers and shoemakers to kings. This traditional firm sold its brand name to Hermès but still runs the London store under its own steam.

George Cleverley Less well known but no less superb. The company's founders made their mark with the look of their bespoke shoes, which have tips shaped rather like a chisel.

Foster & Son In business since 1750, and considered to be one of the oldest surviving shoemakers in London, Foster & Son's workshop is located in Jermyn Street above the store.

Gaziano & Girling They make welted shoes either fully bespoke, made-to-order, or off-the-shelf, with a workshop located in Northampton. Plenty of trunk shows in Europe and USA.

Henry Maxwell Legendary boot and shoemaker, now working under the same roof as Foster & Son in Jermyn Street.

France

Paris attracts visitors from all over the world, and bespoke shoemakers are quick to benefit from this, but there is also domestic demand for handmade shoes from the French capital as well.

John Lobb John Lobb opened a Paris branch in 1902, which has belonged to Hermès since 1976. The bespoke shoes are of the highest quality and some consider them more elegant than those sold in the London branch.

Aubercy Small, less well-known atelier near the stock exchange, with its own style

Around the World

marrying English and Italian elements—so, typically French.

Berluti The reputation that precedes this atelier in the Rue Marbeuf is almost legendary. If you are looking for unusual or even eccentric designs, this is the place for you.

Corthay The Corthay brothers assemble their bespoke and handmade shoes in their own small workshop.

Italy

A lot of clothes are still made by hand south of the Alps, and shoes are no exception. They stand out for their elegance, delicacy, and interesting variations on the standard styles and shapes.

Riccardo Freccia Bestetti A shoemaker based in Vigevano, near Milan, making delicate styles with the occasional extravagant detail as well as more traditional discreet classics.

Gatto Legendary Roman shoemaker who found fame in the 1930s and was taken over in 2007 by Silvano Lattanzi.

Stefano Bemer Bespoke shoemaker whose shoes are made entirely by hand at his workshop in Florence.

Peron & Peron A Bolognese bespoke shoemaker providing the usual classics as well as typically Italian styles with a wider welt.

Silvano Lattanzi His *laboratorio* (workshop) offers both handmade and entirely bespoke models.

Austria

Bálint Viennese shoemaker offering traditional full bespoke and machine-assisted bespoke manufacture. Bálint offers a typical range of styles.

Rudolf Scheer and Sons Probably the most famous Viennese bespoke shoemaker, founded in 1816. Cultivates an exclusive image and the shoes unite elegance and the best fit.

Materna A bespoke shoemaker based in central Vienna whose workshop also produces a compact range of ready-to-wear, handstitched welted shoes.

Maftei A native of Romania who has been making shoes in Vienna under his own name since 1996. Extensive travel has brought him international renown.

A. Novak Opened in 1948 by Leopold Novak and still in family hands. Traditional

Bespoke Shoemakers

Viennese bespoke shoes and also orthopedic footwear.

Petkov Founded in Vienna in 1905 as a repair shop and bespoke shoemaker, now making shoes in the classic Viennese tradition.

Maßschuhmacherei Pfaffenlehner After training with Scheer in Vienna and a subsequent apprenticeship in Venice, Doris Pfaffenlehner opened her workshop near Mariazell in the Austrian Alps.

Haderer Active in Salzburg since 1900, making classic shoes for suits or bespoke Haferl shoes.

Hungary

László Vass Vass was able to carve out a niche for his bespoke shoes during the first decade after the fall of the Iron Curtain and is now continuing a proud Hungarian tradition.

Poland

Jan Kielman Founded in Warsaw in 1883, Jan Kielman's shoemaking business has survived two world wars as well as Communism. It still maintains the old traditions to this day.

Germany

The bespoke shoemaking scene has woken up a little over the last few years, enlivened by a new and knowledgeable clientele that is not prepared to put up with traveling abroad, long waiting times, and inflated prices for its bespoke shoes.

Harai Schuhe The Hungarian Julius Harai opened his workshop in Neumünster in 1947 and over the next few decades went on to shoe the Federal Republic's elite. His son Martin is continuing the tradition.

Himer & Himer Originally located in Baden-Baden, Axel Himer now offers bespoke shoemaking and repairs in Cologne.

Benjamin Klemann After an apprenticeship with Harai and John Lobb in London, Benjamin Klemann opened his own workshop in 1986. A genuine family business, as all his relatives are bespoke shoemakers.

Hans-Joachim Vauk Traditionally made, handstitched bespoke shoes from Schleswig-Holstein. Regular trunk shows at menswear shops right across Germany.

Vickermann & Stoya Founded in 2004 in a takeover of a bespoke workshop in Baden-Baden. Regular fitting days at events and in-store.

Around the World

Japan

It seems that the Japanese excel in any field in which they choose to engage, so it should come as no surprise that bespoke shoes made in Japan are not only on a par with those made by the best European craftsmen but can often outdo them.

Koji Suzuki One of the most sought-after bespoke shoemakers in Japan. After an apprenticeship with Roberto Ugolini in Florence, he returned home to create his own blend of Italian elegance and English solidity. His workshop is in Kobe in western Japan, where a pronounced Western influence on culture and fashion is evident.

Guild of Crafts Founded in Asakusa in 1998 by Chihiro Yamaguchi, who learned his trade in London. His goal was to have bespoke shoes made by a team of highly qualified craftsmen and the range now includes off-the-shelf, handmade, and fully bespoke shoes.

USA

It should not be surprising that a country as large and as rich as the USA should still have bespoke shoemakers. However, they face strong competition from Europe, which still lures a well-heeled clientele.

Perry Ercolino From an Italian family of shoemakers, studied design in Milan and now runs a workshop in Pennsylvania. His shoes clad the feet of businessmen and Hollywood stars alike.

Oliver Moore Bespoke shoemaker's founded in New York in 1878, offering the classic repertoire of welted shoes.

E. Vogel Bespoke riding boots and shoes, based in Manhattan since 1879. Fittings also offered at trunk shows, such as at riding events.

Gregor Thissen on Shoes

....

" Shoes are an essential component of a man's wardrobe. A shoe that doesn't match an outfit can destroy the overall effect completely and even the best suit will not rescue you from a faux pas. On a more positive note, shoes often put the finishing touch to a perfect look.

Good shoes are unfortunately expensive, but the investment pays off. It's better to buy one pair of carefully selected shoes than a whole rack of average ones. It's easy to be fooled if the shoe is new and nicely polished, and you will make a few mistakes, but quality always shows in the end. I have never regretted spending sometimes horrendous amounts on a pair of shoes; they just look better for longer. Choosing the right shoe for the right occasion is also important, of course. Even though the rules are less strict nowadays and you can combine lots of different things, there are still some things that just don't go. If you pay a little attention, however, you'll soon see this. The combination of shoe and belt is absolutely essential for me—there has to be a harmony or an interplay, both in color and in style. I prefer a heavy, solid shoe, probably because I like to keep my two feet on the ground in life. I cannot stand white shoes in town.

Part of the importance of shoes in a man's life is that shoes have been proved to be one of the first things a woman looks at when sizing up a man—I learnt that from my wife. "

....

Gregor Thissen is the owner and CEO of Scabal, a Brussels-based fabric merchant that supplies bespoke tailors and the best suit manufacturers. The company moved over to factory manufacture in the 1970s and is now one of the leading fabric suppliers.

Bespoke Shoes

Bespoke shoes are considered the height of luxury, but they are also the only self-indulgence whose justification is accepted without hesitation by those who can't afford them.

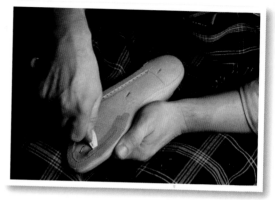

Pretty much everyone thinks a well-fitting shoe is something to aspire to, and for this reason more men are likely to indulge in bespoke shoes than in a handmade suit. I can wear bespoke shoes with jeans, but for a suit I need an occasion or at least some kind of excuse. As not many people know what it feels like to wear a well-fitting bespoke shoe, expectations can vary widely for the newcomer. The most important guide is, of course, the type of shoe that the person usually wears. If you only usually wear sneakers, which wrap the feet in cotton wool, so to speak, you may even be disappointed by how welted shoes made entirely of leather feel. If you are used to wearing welted shoes, however, perhaps even ones that fit well, then the improvement that a made-to-measure pair bring may be disappointingly slight. In this respect, it is quite tricky to describe the "bespoke shoe experience" and elicit realistic expectations.

Nowadays people are familiar with high-tech equipment being used in every area of their lives. Laser measuring devices, for example, are almost standard

issue whenever something has to be measured, such as apartment size. It must be all the more surprising, therefore, when the bespoke shoemaker measures someone's feet with nothing more exotic than a tape measure, and simply makes an outline of the soles with a pencil on a piece of paper. Mechanical aids were used in the 19th century to take footprints, and so on, but many shoemakers have stuck with their traditional tape measures and pencils. All the other data they require to make a last to the right shape come from looking, feeling, and experience.

Before the first pair of bespoke shoes can be made, the lasts must be created. The effort this entails does not have to be repeated for subsequent pairs, provided the client sticks to the same or a similar style. Laced shoes require a different last from slip-on shoes. To compensate for this initial greater expense, some bespoke shoemakers insist on a minimum order of several pairs of shoes. The more famous and sought-after the shoemaker, the greater the minimum order. Other shoemakers charge extra for the last with the first bill. Not all craftsmen pass on the cost in this way, however, and simply rely on the client coming back after the first pair and ordering more shoes.

The bespoke shoemaker at Eduard Meier in Munich makes a shoe completely by hand, on a last that has been made to match the customer's foot exactly and using the best leather and top-quality "accoutrements."

Ignatious Joseph on Shoes

"Europe has inspired a unique fashion culture now respected throughout the world. I do my best to preserve this culture, reinterpreting and reenlivening it with my collections. If we can get young people to be enthusiastic about it, we will have handmade clothes and true elegance in the future. And indeed young people in particular are becoming interested. For me, bespoke shoes are an important part of being a gentleman, a British cultural invention that is now widespread internationally. I grew up in the Commonwealth with afternoon tea, cricket, butlers, and of course the classic British wardrobe, which is why bespoke shoes are not a luxury as far as I am concerned, despite the price. Sometimes only the best is good enough."

Ignatious Joseph is a fashion phenomenon. He is a one-man show, designing and selling the shirts on his luxury Ign. Joseph label all over the world. His personal style has made sure that this "dandy" and gentleman is as famous as his collections, which are sewn in Italy.

Questions

QUESTION: You sometimes see very cheap welted shoes on offer. Can these be any good?

ANSWER: You should first find out for sure if they really are welted shoes and not just an imitation of this style of manufacturing. If they really are welted shoes, do the math: welting is a time-consuming process and if the resulting shoe is relatively cheap, say less than US$130, the manufacturer must have scrimped on the leather and other materials. The upper and lining leather will be of lower quality and the shoes will be fitted with the most basic of soles. Shoes like this are, in the vast majority of cases, a waste of money, as even the most conscientious care cannot make good leather out of bad leather. If you want to buy welted shoes at a good price, have a look for less expensive shoes from better manufacturers in the sales at a good retailer.

QUESTION: Are bespoke shoes really as good as people are always saying?

ANSWER: Bespoke shoes can only be as good as the craftsman who makes them. Not all hairdressers can cut hair well, in just the same way as not all those calling themselves bespoke shoemakers are in fact masters in their field (even if their master craftsman's qualifications suggest otherwise), and you must of course define how

a bespoke shoe is to be judged. Someone who wears welted shoes, where the last is shaped well and the shoes fit well in length and breadth, will notice only a slight improvement in a bespoke shoe, but someone with problematic feet, who has never found a shoe that fits, will find bespoke shoes a revelation. Bespoke shoes are therefore only good if they fit well and have been produced to high standards, even in comparison with a well-made factory shoe.

QUESTION: Is it true that welted shoes are "handmade"?

ANSWER: Salesmen often maintain that welted shoes are handmade. It is not easy to judge the veracity of such a statement, as you first have to define what "handmade" actually means. If it should mean that the shoes have been constructed entirely by hand or with the use of just a few tools, then welted shoes are in no way handmade, i.e. not created entirely by the hand of a craftsman—even he uses a sewing machine for attaching the upper parts together, for example. If "handmade" is defined as meaning that each shoe is assembled individually by hand using machines, then welted shoes are handmade. This is not the most important aspect, however; welted shoes have been made in the same factories using the same machines since the end of the 19th century.

& Answers

It should be noted that a very few work-shops still offer off-the-shelf welted shoes, with soles that are still stitched by hand by a craftsman, as with bespoke shoes, i.e. they are "handstitched."

QUESTION: Is it true that a butler would wear in shoes for his employer?

ANSWER: This tale pops up repeatedly. As it dates back to a time when most well-off gentlemen wore bespoke shoes, any truth in it is likely to be minimal. Why would someone, for whom a particular shoe was not designed to fit, wear in that shoe? It would be superfluous nowadays anyway, as bespoke shoes, if they have been made by a reasonably good craftsman, will fit from the outset.

QUESTION: My last pair of welted shoes seemed narrower than the preceding pair. The retailer said that these are tolerances that I just have to accept with handmade articles. Is this true?

ANSWER: The shoe is made on a last. If it is carved from wood, it is possible that its size may change minimally (for example due to changes of humidity in the workshop). For this very reason, most manufacturers moved over to plastic lasts many years ago, and these lasts do not change at all. Talking about tolerances is not a valid argument; if the shoe is too small, then the size was probably incorrectly noted in the workshop, or the foot size may have changed. This is not as unlikely as it might sound, so it is a good idea to have your feet measured again every so often.

QUESTION: Do expensive welted shoes really last as long as people often say?

ANSWER: You often read about welted shoes that have seen 10, 20, or even 30 years' service. Skepticism and/or further inquiry are probably appropriate in such cases. If two pairs are worn alternately and they really are worn every day or at least five days a week, this will take them to their limits of tolerance at some point. When that might be is a matter of care and maintenance. If you clean your shoes regularly, on average once a week, always use shoe trees, and try not to ask too much of them by continually wearing them in the rain, you will have some 10 or even 15 years of joy from them. During this period, the soles and heels will have to be replaced several times and small repairs to the uppers or the lining will probably be necessary. Most people who wear top-quality shoes switch between several pairs, thus extending their lifespan dramatically.

LEISURE SHOES ARE A GREAT FAVORITE WITH MEN
AND THERE IS A STYLE TO SUIT EVERY TASTE.

Casual Classics

It seems as if the whole world is running around in sneakers or gym shoes, or at least that is the impression you get on the streets of London, Paris, San Francisco, or Tokyo during the warmer months. Look more closely and you will also find a few pairs of high-quality leather shoes, but most people prefer the casual look. One should not decry a desire for comfort in itself, but formal shoes are not unpleasant to wear, so it would appear that "comfort" in this context is less about physical ease and more about a relaxed attitude to life: shoes should fit securely—but not tightly—so that they can be removed in a second and then put on again, without having to fiddle with laces, use a shoe horn, or indeed even bend down.

The absolute antithesis to well-polished lace-ups are flip-flops (also known as thongs)—on the one hand, you have high-quality shoes that need a certain amount of looking after, on the other, cheap footwear made using a minimum of materials that is light and can be put on and taken off effortlessly. Deciding between lace-ups and flip-flops is like choosing between a suit and a T-shirt, between three strenuous weeks of climbing mountains or relaxing on the beach, between learning to play an instrument or just listening to music.

A desire for comfort is not exclusive to this century, but the idea that this kind of demand for ease should be fulfilled at every opportunity is relatively new. When the popular classics of the casual shoe wardrobe were first developed, comfortable or sporty shoes were only worn for "dressing down" or when actually taking part in sporting events.

The home of casual shoe fashions is generally considered to be the USA, and indeed most classic leisure shoes either come directly from America or have their roots there. Europe has its own tradition of informal footwear as well of course, including classics like the sandal, which was worn by young people and eccentrics as a protest shoe in the 1920s and 1930s. The various kinds of canvas shoes with rope soles to be found all around the Mediterranean were popular with beachgoers aiming for a casual look.

The deck shoe is a perfect example of the better kind of leisure shoe, and yet it still represents the polar opposite of the world of work with its strict dress codes. Deck shoe wearers also feel at home in brogues and Oxfords.

The Most

The deck shoe is the classic leisure shoe and one of the few styles in which a man can be confident of not looking ridiculous when sported after finishing work, at the weekend, or during vacations.

There are probably few shoes that are less practical and provide less grip than espadrilles. But who says practical looks good? Espadrilles have the charm of simplicity and spontaneity, and they cover the foot better than flip-flops.

Yes, the penny loafer is indeed a casual shoe, or at least it was invented as such. This classic from the USA is worn in coastal resorts throughout the world with a sport coat and pants or with a suit, but its spiritual home is in a casual combination with chinos.

The saddle shoe is a preppy classic, but most people would recognize shoes with this additional strip of leather as a golf shoe—if they recognized them at all. The saddle shoe joins the penny loafer and the deck shoe as a classic complement to a pair of chinos in the USA.

White or very light shoes are often thought of as rather daring—or even "beyond the pale"—but they are part of the summer uniform in the USA. This isn't a choice to be copied in every circumstance, but they do go rather well with a polo shirt, Bermuda shorts, and a sport coat.

Important Styles

Converse All Stars, perhaps better known as "Chucks," have become the most popular standard leisure shoe over the last few years and are as much a part of the preppy look as they are of casual streetwear.

Those unused to wearing shoes with wedge heels are taking a bit of a risk with clogs, as there is a certain danger of twisting an ankle. There are allegedly people who find these slipper-like creations comfortable and run around in them all day.

Calling sneakers casual shoes would suggest that they were worn only during leisure time—as their inventors intended. Nowadays, however, most men wear traditional leather shoes far less often.

The conservative wearer of welted shoes is unlikely to slip into a pair of flip-flops or sneakers in his leisure time, and on cold or wet days in particular would prefer Veldtschoen-style waterproof lace-ups.

For many people, Birkenstock shoes are completely unacceptable footwear, but nowadays you can turn up practically anywhere in them without raising an eyebrow. This is not necessarily a good thing, but it has made them extremely popular.

House Shoes

House shoes, or house slippers, are a bit like pajamas—most look embarrassing but a few look really stylish. People are entitled to wear whatever they like within the confines of their own four walls—some like to kick back at home in track pants and bathing shoes, others prefer to relax in a robe and leather slippers. House shoes also fulfill a practical function—they keep the floor clean. Dirt and mud from outside stays safely by the door with the shoes, in the lobby, hall or

A grown man in slipper socks is a strange sight, but people living in cold houses might grow to appreciate them; mostly good for children.

English-style leather slippers are also a form of house shoes. Made of very fine leather with a thin sole, they can be very elegant and look almost as good as a real loafer.

The most elegant kind of house shoe is the velvet slipper, which should really be worn with a tuxedo, although it also looks good with corduroy pants and a pullover.

Slippers are not really sexy, but this ancient kind of footwear is entirely suitable for use between the bedroom and the dressing room.

entrance area. House shoes keep your feet warm in cold houses, and to a certain extent they protect you from the injuries that people risk by going barefoot. Anyone who has broken a toe by knocking their foot against some projecting obstacle will soon learn the merits of the house shoe.

House shoes are generally made of three different kinds of materials: fabric, leather, and plastic. The soles of mass-market styles are usually made of plastic—leather soles are the exception rather than the rule. Leather slippers or light slip-on shoes made from leather are more elegant and their light weight makes them ideal to take on journeys. Velvet slippers were never really intended as house shoes, although a lot of people like to wear them as such.

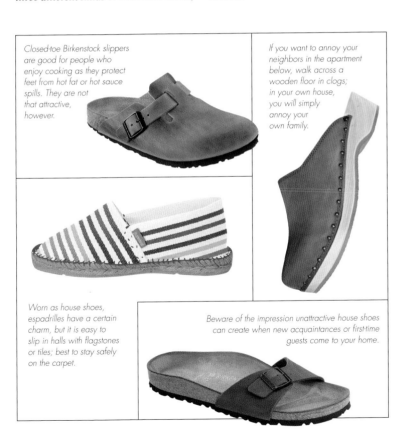

Closed-toe Birkenstock slippers are good for people who enjoy cooking as they protect feet from hot fat or hot sauce spills. They are not that attractive, however.

If you want to annoy your neighbors in the apartment below, walk across a wooden floor in clogs; in your own house, you will simply annoy your own family.

Worn as house shoes, espadrilles have a certain charm, but it is easy to slip in halls with flagstones or tiles; best to stay safely on the carpet.

Beware of the impression unattractive house shoes can create when new acquaintances or first-time guests come to your home.

Sandals

Sandals polarize opinion like no other footwear. While flip-flops may arouse some debate, those who wear them are not condemned as typically middle-class, old before their time, or hippies. Sandals are among the oldest shoe models and, as the typical footwear of the Ancient World, initially came to symbolize high culture. However, they have acquired a negative image that even the fashion designers who trot them out every couple of seasons as a new trend have failed to shift.

The basic idea is of course a good one: straps or bands are used to hold the sole against the foot so it is protected when walking but still permits air to circulate around it. Sandals are pleasant to wear in summer, but their practical advantages have not prevented them from being considered not quite a proper shoe, at least

It is difficult to imagine a greater contrast than that between a modern outdoor sandal and the summer shoe suggested for gentlemen by Dieter Kuckelkorn.

by the standards of most dress codes. A shoe is supposed to cover the foot completely and it is considered a faux pas to reveal socks or bare skin.

This rule might seem outdated, not least as most people turn to flip-flops during the summer, but it still applies. Every summer, magazines discuss the question of whether a man should wear socks with sandals, a practice normally seen as the height of bad taste, but it is often much more comfortable to prevent the soles and straps of a shoe from coming into direct contact with the skin. Aside from the fact that sandals always look a bit suspect, there is nothing to stop you sporting a combination of sock and sandal, but—as we have already suggested—should you be wearing sandals in the first place? Fans of the great outdoors have entirely different opinions of course, wearing their hiking sandals—a modern hybrid of a hiking boot and a sandal—throughout the warm season and often into the fall. One such example is the Teva sandal, which immediately transforms its wearer into a well-traveled son of the soil, even if it is usually worn in urban environments.

Lace-ups in Summer

SOME SHOES ARE SUITABLE FOR HOT DAYS AND STILL ALLOW A MAN TO CUT A DASH.

If you prefer to wear classic clothes in summer as well, you cannot generally go wrong by selecting a classic suit and a shirt. Light wool, linen, silk, or cotton all make for extremely airy suit fabrics, and some shirts have qualities that can even make extreme heat bearable. A gentleman is likely to find little or no alternative to the classic lace-up, however.

Light, suede leather that is dust-proof is often the only concession to the warmer weather. You can also find lace-ups with uppers that come equipped with tiny airholes, or shoes made from woven leather— a somewhat more closed-up alternative to the sandal, and a classic of Continental European elegance, such as the pair shown here by Ludwig Reiter, for example.

Birkenstock: a Very German Brand

The change of image that the Birkenstock brand has undergone is astonishing; in the 1980s, some people would have considered it completely unthinkable to be spotted in these shoes and sandals, but Birkenstock footwear is now as normal and everyday as sorting your recycling or using sustainable resources. Birkenstocks were once almost a byword for peace-loving, ecological types and health freaks, and anyone who didn't vote Green wouldn't have been seen dead in them. These healthy clogs are now considered to be trendy, at least by the models, designers, and film stars who wear them publicly and don't feel they need to sport them only in secret at home or in the safety of their garden.

The Birkenstock company can look back on a long history that saw them celebrating 225 years of the firm's existence in 1999.

Konrad Birkenstock, a specialist shoe retailer, began manufacturing shoe lining inserts in 1869 and promoted his ideas for perfectly fitting shoes to clients in Germany and Austria on numerous lecture tours until the First World War. The family firm experienced considerable growth in the 1920s and 1930s as a result of the training courses it provided for retailers, and, with the Second World War over, the book *Podiatric System Birkenstock*, published in 1947, went on to enjoy enormous success. The decades of the 1950s, 60s, and 70s saw Birkenstock develop pioneering innovations such as footprint impression paper that changed color to show the exact shape of the foot, malleable thermo-cork (BirkoKork), and an electromagnetic shaping machine. The thong sandal was launched on the market in 1982, proving a great success, and since 1988 these have been produced with solvent-free adhesive, despite

the considerably higher costs and extra technical challenges this represents.

Environmental considerations are also important in the manufacture of the linings, with energy use reduced by 90 percent, according to the firm's figures. Such an ecologically friendly image seems to suit Birkenstock, and locating their production facilities in Germany, thereby avoiding long transportation from countries with lower wages, is also part of this approach. Besides adidas and PUMA, Birkenstock is one of the most famous German shoe brands in the world, and even domestically the manufacturer is seen to be at the forefront of the industry. While Gucci might be the first name to spring to mind when one is asked to identify an Italian brand, Germany is most associated with sports and health shoes. This is certainly telling, but not necessarily a bad thing—and is in line with the modern German belief that they have the most prominent profile and boast the most solid success in these fields.

Materials and Processing

THE RAW MATERIALS USED IN BIRKENSTOCKS MEET STRINGENT STANDARDS IN EVERY DETAIL.

SOLES
The inventor of the first flexible deep-profile cork lining now offers a variety of different soles: the classic models have a supportive cork inner sole for maximum comfort, protected by a slightly flexible and hardwearing outer sole.

BUCKLES
These are handled repeatedly during the life of a shoe, coming into contact with sweat, fat, water, and dust. In order to survive such trials, the buckles (all made in-house) are stainless and have several layers of stove-enameling.

LEATHER
A number of different kinds of leather are used, including velour, suede and other napped leathers, smooth leather, and varieties with an embossed or natural surface. There is also a variety of fabrics and exclusive, patented materials.

Bathing Shoes

The term "bathing shoes" describes the waterproof footwear worn in showers and saunas or beside swimming pools to protect feet from dirt and slipping. Bathing shoes can now be worn with increasing confidence beyond the wet room or pool.

Dark blue flip-flops: the maritime variant.

Slightly more padding with a thicker sole.

Brazil's national footwear.

Chocolate brown, a bestseller in summer.

The plastic sandal in particular, better known as the flip-flop or thong, has experienced an astounding change in its use and image. Once a cheap, disposable shoe acquired on vacation and then stashed away with your beach towel until the following summer, it has now become an essential fashionable accessory. Wearing bathing shoes simply for swimming has become the exception rather than the rule these days, and saving these rubber classics for the beach or the pool is often seen as an attempt to appear rather eccentric.

The Adilette Since 1972

ORIGINALLY WORN ONLY BY SPORTS ENTHUSIASTS, ADILETTES ARE NOW STARS IN THEMSELVES.

Adidas is one of the brands that has undergone an astonishing transformation over the last few decades. The name has stood for quality since its very beginnings, but the sports shoes from Herzogenaurach in Germany initially had very little to do with lifestyle and absolutely nothing to do with glamour—sports fans wore adidas to play sports. As leisurewear increasingly raided the sportswear wardrobe during the 1980s, the barriers between the two styles of clothing were broken down, and the same thing happened with footwear. Sneakers became more and more popular as general leisure shoes, and bathing shoes—which had been considered a necessary evil for decades— slowly worked their way up to becoming objects of fashion. By the time Madonna was appearing in

public in these striped, plastic, open-toed mules with a solid sole, people were beginning to look at Adilettes in a new light. They had faithfully served a host of amateur and professional soccer stars since 1972 and were now appropriated by trendsetters being seen about town, visiting clubs, or even performing onstage—something that did no harm to their popularity with the general public, which may also have had something to do with their cheapness and solidity.

The Simple Life

There is nothing new about the idea of shedding your everyday clothes and dressing in a more simple and modest style in given situations—pilgrims have been doing it for centuries. When people attempt this on vacation, they appear to adopt another persona along with their less fussy clothes.

Journeys that served no economic purpose, in other words journeys of discovery or for leisure, were the preserve of the wealthy well into the 19th century, and a lack of money and time meant that even in the early 20th century, most ordinary workers could not afford a vacation. Getting away from home for a short period only really became an affordable prospect for the man in the street after the Second World War. From the 18th to the 19th century, however, the rich followed the tradition of the Grand Tour, an extended journey principally through

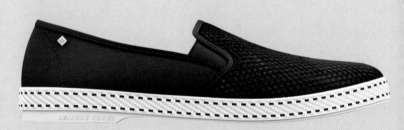

Rivieras beach shoes in dark blue go perfectly with light chinos and a polo shirt.

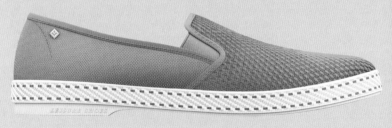

This sun-drenched color reflects the warm hues of the south of France, where they are summer classics.

the southern reaches of Europe, viewed as the culmination of a young man's education.

In the 1920s, the upper classes were already habitual travelers, with the trips being much longer than those undertaken by modern rich globetrotters, although the means of transport were not quite as speedy. In Europe, beach vacations in the south of France and Italy were especially popular and the celebrities of the day would exchange a stiff collar, hat, and suit for airy clothing and simple shoes. The outfits drew their inspiration from the work clothes of fishermen or farmers—in an idealized form, of course. A duke or a captain of industry could therefore take a stroll along the quayside in a striped, collarless shirt, flared, belted pants, and simple linen shoes with rope soles before dropping in somewhere for an aperitif.

This swapping of roles and clothing could be observed all over Europe: the English transforming into Scots to go hunting on Highland moors, Berlin magnates turning into mountain peasants at the first whiff of summer, and elegant Parisians enjoying their vacations *à la Provençale*.

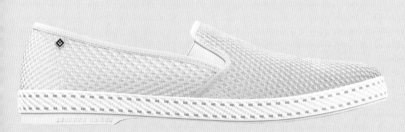

Light fabric shoes in pale sandy shades from France are particularly good for the beach.

This fiery red makes a strong statement and complements linen pants and red and white striped T-shirts.

Espadrilles

Espadrilles by [espadrij] are made in many different colors in a factory located in the French Pyrenees.

The raw materials are stored in the factory building; the fabrics used for the uppers and soles are all made under one roof.

Jute soles waiting to be attached to an upper of tough sailcloth, either by hand or by machine.

One collection of espadrilles is always finished by hand, while another is finished using a sewing machine.

The key element of the sole is the jute fiber, which is spun before being made into a sole. A natural rubber sole protects them from moisture.

The upper is cut to a variety of sizes from templates; lasts are not used for these shoes.

in the Making

Most espadrilles are manufactured in Asia, but [espadrij] make sure theirs are produced in France and Spain.

You don't need much more than a needle to make genuine espadrilles and the manufacturing process has not changed in centuries.

The rope part of the sole consists of a plaited ribbon of jute that is carefully coiled into place. Meticulous work is required here.

The tools and production methods used to make espadrilles have become a popular tourist attraction, even in the Pyrenees.

Espadrilles are made for sunny days and despite having rubber soles, these lightweight fabric and jute shoes are not suitable for rainy weather.

A finished example from the [espadrij] collection. A southern European classic, just like olive oil, wine or cheese.

Questions

QUESTION: Can I wear penny loafers without socks in the summer?

ANSWER: There's no rule saying you cannot wear penny loafers or similar slip-ons without socks in your leisure time, and some people even think it is a particularly smart and cosmopolitan look. A lot of men are not excessively keen on wearing shoes with bare feet, however, and sneaker socks—beloved of many sneakers wearers—consequently stick out of the top of many slip-on styles and so are out of the question. This means you have the choice of learning to enjoy wearing shoes with bare feet or putting some socks on—it's more comfortable anyway.

QUESTION: Are sneakers suitable as everyday shoes?

ANSWER: An orthopedic expert would probably answer this question differently from the spokesperson for a sneakers manufacturer. The man in the street might think that sneakers couldn't do harm as they are soft and don't cramp the foot; they are in essence sports shoes and must therefore be healthy. On the other hand, no one would dream of strolling through a pedestrian zone wearing soccer boots. There are specialized shoes for every kind of sport; these have been developed for a purpose and are not intended for everyday use. So are sneakers viable? As long as they provide enough support and don't cramp the foot, there is not much to say against them, although they generally don't grip the foot very securely as the uppers are manufactured from soft materials. There is also the problem of their breathability. For this reason, stick to leather shoes for long-term use, preferably of a superior manufacturing style.

QUESTION: I always get sweaty feet in sneakers; why is that?

ANSWER: A lot of men think that sweaty feet are as much a part of maleness as growing a beard or fancying a beer, but heavy foot perspiration is a real problem for many men. Whether sweaty feet smell or not is determined by your socks and shoes—most sneakers are made predominantly from synthetic materials and the foot cannot help sweating in them. Even sneakers that are made from breathable fabrics will cause foot perspiration and odor on hot days. If you don't wish to wear leather shoes, at least make sure that your socks are made of natural fibers (cotton—or wool is even better) and that you give your sneakers plenty of time to air. Leather shoes are always worth a try, however—there are plenty of people who have suffered from sweaty feet for years and been cured overnight by good leather shoes.

& Answers

QUESTION: Are flip-flops healthy for your feet?

ANSWER: In warm weather, flip-flops have one key advantage, which is that your feet are ventilated from all sides as you walk, although the soles of your feet will sweat heavily in plastic styles if you stand around for too long. The disadvantages of flip-flops are that they provide no support or protection for the foot, and they often lead to foot cramps—when they are too big, wearers tend to grip on to them with their toes. They are certainly pleasant to wear on the beach or in the country as an alternative to a constricting shoe and are also healthier, but they are not suitable for long-term use, however.

QUESTION: Deck shoes are classics and currently back in fashion. Are they recommended from a health point of view?

ANSWER: The original deck shoes such as Sperry Topsiders were only intended for use on the deck of sailboats; their soles are very thin and thus do not absorb the impact of taking a step. Their moccasin-style construction means that the upper material cramps the toes, which is not ideal either. Deck shoes are not suitable for long-term use in urban environments but, as they are made of leather and usually have a thin leather inner sole, they are preferable to sneakers in terms of minimizing sweating. The manufacturers of deck shoes are, of course, aware of the limitations of the style and for this reason stock a wide range of similar models with thicker outer soles and supportive inner soles. These models are much better suited for use as an everyday shoe.

QUESTION: I like wearing sandals. Do I have to wear socks with them?

ANSWER: Italian newspapers have a field day every year, mocking tourists from northern and central Europe for their sock and sandal combinations, and the most likely offenders tend to be the German, British, Dutch, Swiss, Austrians, and Scandinavians. Sandals only look good in the rarest of cases, so it is difficult to say whether socks really improve or detract from their appearance. A lot of men fail to take very good care of their feet, and in such cases socks can be a valuable cover-up. Devotees of sandals should therefore look after their feet and stay loyal to their favorite shoes, with or without socks. Others should remember that there are much better-looking leisure shoes out there. If you like a sporty look, you might consider branching out into hiking shoes, classic fans could try deck shoes or penny loafers, and fashion victims could wear linen sneakers.

WHETHER USED FOR SPORT OR JUST AS SHOES FOR DAILY
WEAR, SNEAKERS CAN BE SEEN EVERYWHERE.

Sneakers

Sneakers are a personal statement about life, just like jeans. When you pull on a pair of Chucks, you are wearing a legend, even if in fact what you are actually putting on is just a pair of ankle-high linen boots with rubber soles that give you sweaty feet in summer and frozen toes in winter. As far as the fit, lifespan, and environment for the foot are concerned, sneakers perform considerably less well than comparable shoes in leather. Their fans would not disagree, but who needs to speak up in defense of sneakers? People wear them because—for sneakers enthusiasts at least—there is simply no alternative.

Sneakers were originally called sports shoes and there are still plenty of different names in the English language for them. In Germany they were originally known as "gym shoes," but this term applies to sneakers about as well as "dance hall" does to a club. The majority of sneakers are never worn for sports and certainly not in the gym. Sneakers are about as sporty as a sports car, and are often worn by people who engage in very little athletic endeavor.

The history of sneakers, just like jeans, goes back to the 19th century, an era which, when viewed from a modern perspective, is seen as being defined by its formality, stiff manners, and constrictive clothing. However, the 19th century was also an era of industrialization and it witnessed the birth of popular culture. Factories made shoes and clothes for ever wider sections of society, and mass production allowed them to keep pace with the rapidly growing populations of the cities.

The two most important branches of the now extremely disparate sneaker family are the simple rubber-soled leisure shoe made from fabric, and the genuine sports shoe. Vans were designed as casual footwear from the outset, for example, and were intended to last well and look cool. The adidas brand, on the other hand, comes from the world of sport and remains most at home there to this day. These two lines of descent have given birth to a range of styles, but the heritage is sometimes difficult to establish precisely, if at all—there have always been pure leisure sneakers and pure sports shoes, but it is the hybrid styles that dominate.

Once simply known as gym shoes, sneakers are the shoe of choice for everyday wear for old and young alike in many families. However, their comfort comes complete with a number of disadvantages.

The Big

adidas

Founded in 1949 by the Dassler brothers, who had been making sports shoes since the 1920s. There is now a complete range for sports and fashion, but old styles dating from the 1960s, 70s, and 80s in particular have attained cult status.

ASICS

Kihachiro Onitsuka has been making sports shoes in Japan since 1949 and the company has been called ASICS since 1977. The old-school models from the 1960s are now legendary, as their fame has grown in recent years.

Converse

Converse Chucks are probably the best-known sneakers in the world. They were originally designed as proper basketball boots and enjoyed great success as such before becoming leisure shoes.

Dunlop

Dunlop was founded in Australia in 1924 to produce gum boots and canvas shoes with rubber soles. The Volley style, released in 1939, was worn by some of the most successful tennis players of the next 40 years. The firm concentrates on canvas sneakers.

Fila

An Italian sportswear label that originally specialized in sports underwear. Founded in Biella in 1911, it now offers a full range that includes sports shoes and sneakers. The brand achieved cult status in the 1980s.

Gola

Every country in Europe has its cult sneaker brand, and in the UK it is probably Gola. Founded in 1905, it is reputedly the oldest sportswear brand in the country. The heart of the collection comprises soccer boots and running shoes, with leisure sneakers also gaining in popularity in recent years.

K-Swiss

Founded by Swiss brothers in the USA in 1966, the company achieved legendary status by producing the first American leather tennis shoe. One of the most successful US footwear, sports shoe, and sneakers brands.

Keds

Keds canvas gym shoes have been around in the USA since 1916, although success in Europe is a more recent phenomenon. In the 1980s, Keds were known to only a few insiders as a typical preppy shoe.

Brands

Künzli

A traditional manufacturer founded in Switzerland in 1927, initially as a supplier to K-Swiss. Immediately identifiable by their five "little blocks" logo, the range now includes genuine sports shoes and sneakers. Also manufactures therapeutic shoes made to treat sports injuries.

Le Coq Sportif

A French sportswear label whose roots stretch back to the 19th century. Has worked closely with adidas since the 1960s and was taken over by the German company in 1974. After weathering a few storms, the firm was relaunched in 2005 with sportswear and sneakers.

New Balance

New Balance developed from a producer of orthopedic footbeds and is now one of the biggest running and sports shoe manufacturers in the USA. Pioneering running shoe models have made the brand popular for sneakers as well.

Nike

The label, with its famous "swoosh" logo, was founded in the USA as Blue Ribbon Sports in 1964, initially importing Onitsuka Tiger shoes until its own creations first hit the market in 1972. The Nike brand has strong links with basketball.

Puma

Puma was founded by Rudolf Dassler in 1948 and is now one of the largest providers of sporting goods. It attained its fame principally with soccer boots, but the old sports shoe models dating from the 1960s and 1970s are popular worn as sneakers.

Reebok

This typical 1980s brand focused on women's fitness. Their original, refined image as British producers of expensive quality shoes is now largely forgotten. The Classic model in black and white has achieved classic status in its field for Reebok.

Vans

The brand was founded in California in 1966, so it remains one of the more junior US sneaker manufacturers. The focus has been on making shoes for leisure, skating, and everything connected with California. The style with the black and white checkerboard pattern has become legendary.

Michael Michalsky on Shoes

....

" Shoes make an outfit cool, perfect—or sometimes, a catastrophe. The rules today are of course different from those of 25 years ago; in fact, there are hardly any 'dress rules' now and whether something works or not depends largely on the individual and their personal style. This is definitely linked to the triumphant arrival of the sneaker, which nowadays are as much of a status symbol as handmade classic shoes. I would describe my own shoe style as 'eclectic' and 'taken out of context': I like wearing sneakers with classic items, for example, or I combine classic styles—made with unusual materials or in unusual colors and worn without socks—with casual sportswear. Shoes are my greatest passion and I can't walk past a good shoe shop—even though I am not a woman. "

....

The German designer Michael Michalsky was head designer at Levi's and adidas before starting his own label in Berlin. His collections combine modernity and everyday suitability with the greatest elegance. In addition to fashion, Michalsky also designs furniture and interiors.

Basic Shapes

The range of sneakers on the market nowadays is just so vast that it is difficult to keep track of them all; but try to see past the colors, styles, and variety of materials used and it will be easy to spot the basic models that underpin them. Most are based on patterns dating back to the sneaker's earliest origins, from the late 19th century to the 1950s, or have their roots in genuine sports shoes—footwear designed to fulfill a specific function for a particular activity.

The most basic form, the mother of all other sneakers, is the Oxford pattern in canvas with a rubber sole. Shoes like this first appeared as boots and half-shoes at the end of the 19th century, when they were popular for sporting activities such as croquet, tennis, badminton, and cycling. This original form was followed by linen gym shoes such as those made by Keds for young women and children in the 1950s. Sailcloth tennis shoes with rubber soles, as worn from the 1930s to the 1970s, are another close relative.

SOCCER SHOES were originally stitched from leather because of the heavy wear

(Below) Indoor soccer boots that are also sports shoe models are among the most popular sneakers today.

(Above) Wearing a bowling shoe on the street is in some respects a contradiction in terms, but sneakers with bowling shoe styling share only their outward appearance with the original shoe used for bowling.

they were subjected to in the game; boots were gradually superseded by half-shoes. The leather often got wet and would only keep its suppleness through careful and regular maintenance; even so, it would eventually become stiff and inflexible. The field variety is unsuitable as a leisure shoe because of the studs on its soles, so the indoor version has broken through as a leisure shoe.

BOWLING SHOES are also one of the most basic forms taken on by sneakers. There is a myriad of different kinds, although the early versions were generally made from leather and had perforations for ventilation. They thus resembled classic cycling shoes (whose stiff sole was perfect for pedaling but got in the way of walking) and sneaker designers drew inspiration from this look as well.

BASKETBALL BOOTS The early versions—ankle-height with rubber soles—are one of the most popular styles ever. These were originally worn just to play the sport but later-generation basketball boots, generally made of leather, have also become popular as sneakers.

CANVAS SLIP-ON SHOES such as those by Vans have arisen with no sports background and were soon discovered by the skateboarding community, even though they had been intended as general leisure shoes.

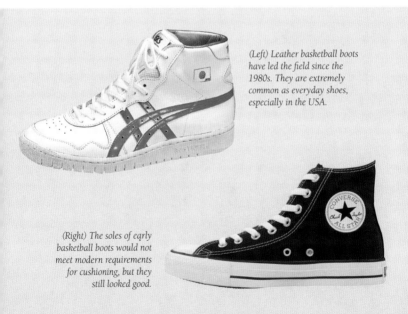

(Left) Leather basketball boots have led the field since the 1980s. They are extremely common as everyday shoes, especially in the USA.

(Right) The soles of early basketball boots would not meet modern requirements for cushioning, but they still looked good.

The Greatest Classics

All classic sneakers are mass-produced, although this does not mean that every style is available in great numbers or is even still available; over the years there have been exclusive and extremely expensive limited editions produced for special occasions, and this remains the case today. In 2005, for example, adidas

The Nite Jogger, adidas' first model, was launched in 1962 as a soccer boot for frozen pitches. The style was slightly redesigned in 1970, but the original design is still the most popular.

A running legend: Tom Fleming won the New York City Marathon in a pair of New Balance 320s in 1975 and in 1976 the model was hailed as the best running shoe on the planet by Runner's World.

produced an anniversary edition, crafted from the finest leather, for the 35th birthday of its Superstar model; the shoe came packaged with various care products and a golden shoe horn in a white leather box with gold fittings.

The total number of sneakers that have been launched on the market and sold is now so enormous it is beyond count. Distilling from this a list of the best or the most important would be just as difficult, a bit like choosing the best wines of all time. The styles listed here are therefore a subjective selection—every sneaker fan has a list of his personal favorites, of course.

The adidas Superstar was the first lowtop basketball shoe on the market in 1970. With its rubber toecap, the design is unmistakable.

The best-known modern basketball boot design is probably the Nike Air Jordan. The first model to be made available for sale to the public appeared in 1985, although Michael Jordan had been wearing them since 1984.

Designer Sneakers

The term "designer sneakers" seems rather strange in some respects; as such it is reminiscent of the designer jeans that were a passing and questionable fad in the 1980s. Sneakers are really defined by being cheap. There are sneakers that are marketed at inflated prices, of course, but the basic concept is clear; transforming sneakers into a luxury product is a contradiction in terms. On the other hand, you might question whether it isn't time to take over the basic form of the sneaker, and adopt its chief selling point—its comfort (or more precisely

(Right) Extreme luxury. A pair of bespoke sneakers made by Vickermann & Stoya. (Above) Even in the 1990s, Santoni was leading the field in making designer sneakers. The Italian manufacturer also makes sneaker models for famous luxury brands.

its suppleness)—and create a shoe that has none of the disadvantages of the cheap sneaker?

Or to put it another way: if you don't like wearing plastic on your feet and are not keen on getting sweaty feet, are you condemned to have to give up the various merits and advantages of sneakers? This is exactly the approach of the companies offering a better class of sneaker; in other words, footwear that is acceptable to the kind of man who has been spoilt by welted shoes. The idea came about in the 1990s in the wake of the trend for smart-casual fashion—luxury goods manufacturers were looking for the next big thing for their demanding clientele and also needed something to offer young men with deep pockets. What better idea than to exploit their love of sneakers by producing designer versions of bowling boots, cycling shoes, soccer boots, and other sporting footwear from the 1950s, 60s, and 70s. Shoes like these have since become firm favorites in the smart-casual wardrobe.

THE LINE BETWEEN SPORTS SHOES AND EVERYDAY SHOES IS BECOMING INCREASINGLY BLURRED.

Sports Shoes

A good way to make a comparison between leisure sneakers and sports shoes is to use an analogy from the world of automobiles, in which case sneakers would be something like a sporty coupe, not unlike a VW Golf, whereas a sports shoe would be a touring car or a Formula 1 racer. The comparison is not entirely appropriate, however—you can do a certain amount of physical exercise in everyday sneakers, while a number of the key qualities now considered essential for proper sports shoes in terms of breathability and low weight were not available to athletes at all a few decades ago, but that didn't stop records being broken.

Sports shoes reflect the parameters of contemporary shoe production for the era in which they were produced: in the late 19th century, croquet and tennis shoes were made from sailcloth with a rubber sole, while nowadays the upper is woven from artificial fibers or made of synthetic leather. The first sports shoes were often made by athletes or sports stars themselves, either independently or in close cooperation with shoe manufacturers, rather than by a manufacturer attempting to anticipate the needs of athletes or trying to produce a range to make sport fashionable. The first real sports shoes—and this is especially true of running shoes—were created by people who knew exactly what they wanted but weren't able to find it.

The reinvention of genuine sports shoes as leisure shoes—partially a retro movement that latched on to the charms of the styles from the 1970s and 1980s—led to a combining of the sports shoe with the aesthetics of leisure footwear. A genuine indoor soccer shoe from 1979 can be seen as the forerunner of a leisure shoe that is intended to be worn purely on the street. That any consideration for the health of the foot may then sometimes be left behind in the locker room, to use an entirely appropriate metaphor, should come as no surprise. Shoes that are constructed for short-term use in a sporting context are not necessarily suitable for long-term use as street shoes.

Golf is a sporting discipline that has inspired a number of fashions in smart-casual wear. Golfing fashion has retained its preppy styling despite all the trends toward increased functionality.

A Shoe for Every Sport

Different sports have different footwear requirements, so specialist sports shoes were a very early development, and indeed a huge range of specialized sports shoes have been designed since the end of the 19th century. Some of these are really only suitable for their particular purpose; the best example of this is the classic cycling shoe, which is unsuitable for everyday use because of its stiff sole.

A few sports shoes have become popular as street shoes, such as indoor soccer shoes, basketball boots, or even bowling shoes.

Indoor soccer and the traditional, open-air game are quite different sports and the boots are different too. There are no studs on the indoor version and the upper is particularly breathable.

Boxers need especially light, nonslip footwear so they can "float like a butterfly," but they also need plenty of grip when they "sting like bees"; the material of choice for the upper is thus something light, strong, and synthetic.

Adidas call this hybrid shoe/sandal a "shandal": it is intended for outdoor activities on a wide range of surfaces.

Sprinters don't wear leather shoes these days, they would be too heavy; the preference is for shoes with removable spikes made from superlight synthetic materials.

Handball players are very quick around the court and wear special sports shoes for this lightning-fast sport, which support the foot when jumping and running.

Wrestling boots have to have plenty of grip and provide support for the ankle; nevertheless, the upper allows the athlete plenty of room for movement.

This is what shoes for competitive dancers look like now; functionality has overtaken any aesthetic traditions in this activity as well.

Basketball Boots

In Europe, basketball has never acquired the popularity that the sport enjoys in the USA, but all kinds of basketball boots have become enormously popular as leisure-wear. This is perhaps because however popular soccer may be, only the indoor type of soccer boot, such as the adidas Samba, can be worn as leisure wear. The basketball boot had already achieved global reach and renown in its original form, the All Star by Converse, and by the end of the 1960s, this model had cornered the basketball boot market in the USA, with Converse still enjoying a market share of 90 percent in 1967. It is said that 250 million pairs of the All Star had been sold by the time it was edged out of the game by leather styles. A keen sales war flared up between the various manufacturers during the 1970s, with the deciding factor always being attributed to the success of one particular player in one particular shoe. In 1983 there was a new turn of events: Nike brought out the Air Force 1 model, the first shoe with an air cushion sole, and this and ensuing models assured it pole position over the next few years. The success of this shoe as leisurewear was also linked with Michael Jordan, who had worn Nike from the beginning of his career: the shoe models sold under the name of this extremely successful and globally famous sports star brought the company billions of dollars in profits.

Ultimately, Nike even created a personal imprimatur for the superstar, the

Onitsuka's basketball boots still have much in common with their American predecessors.

Jordan brand. Reebok, Nike's great competitor, had a hit with its Pump style in 1989. The shoe was equipped with inflatable air cushions that could support and stabilize the foot as required, and original examples from this period are now cult shoes. Nike fought back with similar technology, but the results failed to live up to expectations. Its Air Jordan styles continued to be very popular, however, with the launch of new models invariably attended by vast crowds and even the occasional scuffle. Countries around the world were assigned a maximum number of pairs of these sneakers, with some only being awarded as few as a dozen. If you look at today's top Nike models—some of which come with an iPhone app to increase the effectiveness of the wearer's training regime—and then compare these with a pair of Chucks All Stars, you might be amused by the latter's relative simplicity; it used to be just as much fun to play basketball in modest canvas boots, and the achievements of the athletes were just as impressive. Ultimately, technique, talent, and perseverance count for far more than the shoes.

The Cool Tigers

ONITSUKA BEGAN MAKING SPORTS SHOES IN 1949, BECOMING ASICS IN 1977.

Stripes are as much a part of sports shoes as perforations are for brogues; stripes are easily recognizable from a distance and they also add stability to the upper. In addition to being the distinguishing feature of certain famous shoes from Germany, stripes—admittedly in a different arrangement—are also a feature on Onitsuka's famous Tigers. When Kihachiro Onitsuka took his first faltering steps into the sports shoe business in Japan after the end of the Second World

War, there was no hint of the modern preoccupation with sneakers as all-round shoes: Onitsuka was interested in sport, not lifestyle. Basketball boots were the first port of call, closely followed by shoes for sprinters, with the Limber model coming out in 1966 for the run-up to the Olympic Games in Mexico in 1968. The style is now better known as the Mexico 66 and while not viable as a sports shoe today, it has held its own as a multifunction retro sneaker.

Golf Shoes—High-tech with Tradition

Any non-golfer browsing a large golf retailer's catalog or website might be surprised at the range of products available, the subtle detail of the equipment, and the variety of models and colors on offer: they would be amazed to read about special leather uppers, tanned exclusively for the manufacturer and guaranteed to be waterproof even without a membrane, polyurethane inner linings offering comfort and the best cushioning, or perhaps sole inserts made from EVA (ethylene vinyl acetate), providing a soft and nonstick surface for the foot. There is even

The two-tone saddle shoe is the basic model for many golf shoes, although it may also come equipped with a brogue wing tip.

There is a wide variety of possible leather and color combinations, as the range offered by US manufacturer Allen Edmonds shows.

a product designed to support the middle part of the instep to give the foot additional stability during the swing and play in general.

However, if you look at the basic golf shoe, pure and simple, mentally removing all the extra high-tech elements, the high-tech impression is stripped away and the shoe is not actually that special—only mentioned here as the reader may not be aware of it. You then ask—as is the case with many modern sports shoes—how the sportsmen and women of yesteryear were capable of what we still regard as

great performances in their simple footwear made of leather or canvas. It is crucial that golf shoes are waterproof as the players are always standing around on grass, which of course can be damp or

A golf shoe has to grip the foot, and for this reason, the welted shoe manufacturing process is particularly suitable for this kind of sports shoe.

The soles of golf shoes must allow the player to find a secure footing in the grass of the course and they must also be waterproof.

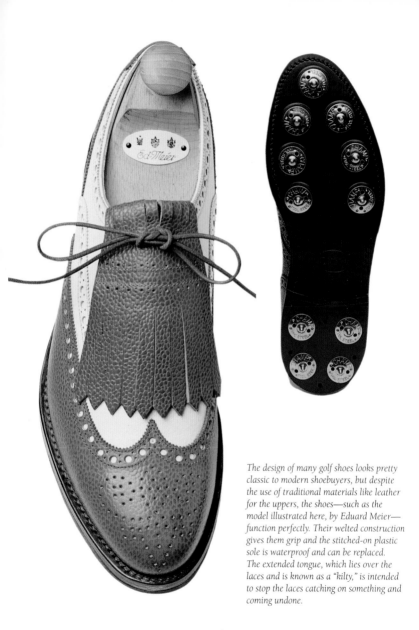

The design of many golf shoes looks pretty classic to modern shoebuyers, but despite the use of traditional materials like leather for the uppers, the shoes—such as the model illustrated here, by Eduard Meier— function perfectly. Their welted construction gives them grip and the stitched-on plastic sole is waterproof and can be replaced. The extended tongue, which lies over the laces and is known as a "kilty," is intended to stop the laces catching on something and coming undone.

wet. The waterproofing must be guaranteed for the soles as well as the welt and on all sides of the upper.

In the early 20th century, when Goretex and other synthetic materials had yet to be invented, leather golf shoes were vegetable-tanned and then treated with special coating waxes to make them waterproof. To prevent these usually welted shoes from admitting water from the side, between the welt and the upper, so-called "piping" was inserted. The leather outer soles were initially protected from water with special tanning before leather soles gave way to rubber ones. The foot obtained grip through the tight hold on the instep, thanks to the shoe's construction, and the correspondingly firm anchoring of the heel cap. The extras offered today are no doubt useful and helpful, but any improvement on the traditional golf shoe made with a welted construction could not be described as particularly significant. The design of golf shoes is now much more oriented toward the look of leisure sneakers and shoes worn for other kinds of sports, although some golf shoe designs are still reminiscent of classic "saddle shoes" or "brogues," and the two-tone color scheme made possible by the cut of the vamp panels in both models is still as popular as ever.

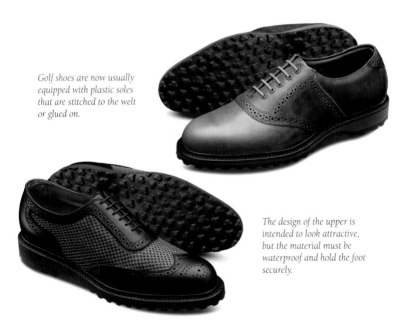

Golf shoes are now usually equipped with plastic soles that are stitched to the welt or glued on.

The design of the upper is intended to look attractive, but the material must be waterproof and hold the foot securely.

Ebbo Tücking on Shoes

"While I swear by classic welted shoes for my business footwear, I am aware of the importance of new technologies for sports. As a passionate jogger I make sure the cushioning is good and thus don't wear my shoes for more than a year. My oldest, well-loved business shoes are nigh on 20 years old, however."

Prof. Dr. Ebbo Tücking is one of the founders and equity partners in Cove & Co., gentlemen's outfitters. Their range includes tailored garments, bespoke suits, accessories, and top-quality shoes. He is particularly appreciative of the craftsmanship associated with bespoke clothing and so the company employs no fewer than 70 tailors in the workshops of its 11 branches.

Running Shoes

When sneakers fans talk about "old school," they mean the sports shoes and training kit of the 1960s and 1970s. The history of the running shoe does not stretch much further back than this, or at least that's where the history of such industrially produced footwear begins. This may come as some surprise, given that humans have been able to run from the very beginning and that running must have been some kind of competitive act for almost as long. Reaching the finish line barefoot, as some top athletes occasionally do today—indeed, sometimes even well ahead of the field—was also how the first athletes ran. There is certainly something to be said for running shoes, however—they protect the soles of the feet and cushion each step, although the cushioning property has only really come into its own since people have started running on hard surfaces such as roads and tracks.

The pioneers of industrial running shoe production come from Germany and Japan; the shoe designer Eugen Brütting, the Dassler brothers, and Kihachiro Onitsuka. The Dasslers initially worked together before parting ways and founding the firms of adidas and PUMA—and "the rest is history," you might say. Onitsuka began in Japan by making basketball boots before turning his attention to other kinds of sports, including running. At the heart of all the innovations in running shoe technology was the cushioned middle sole, as seen in the Achill model brought out by adidas in 1968. Eugen Brütting launched his Roadrunner model—now a legend and still in production—in 1970, providing more room

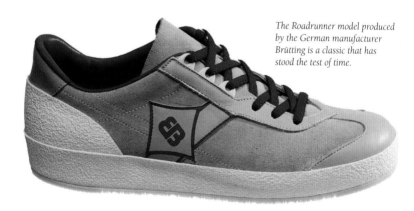

The Roadrunner model produced by the German manufacturer Brütting is a classic that has stood the test of time.

for the toes with a rounded cap and an upper made of soft, suede leather.

The asymmetrical last used to make the Roadrunner is known as a sickle mold. The shoe does not taper toward the center and the big toe is thus not squashed. For early running fans—there was no talk of jogging in those days—the Achill and Roadrunner amounted to a great improvement; people had previously run in normal sports shoes that had no cushioning to speak of. Adidas improved the shoes continuously over the next few years with models such as the Formula 1, TRX or SL72, SL74, and SL76. US firms of the time, such as Etonic or New Balance, were principally producing shoes for the domestic market. Nike was registered as a trademark in 1971 and the firm behind it, Blue Ribbon Sports, founded in 1964, had been marketing Onitsuka shoes in the USA before starting its own collection. It was the tennis stars of the 1970s who helped to make Nike famous, but the firm also made a name for itself with running shoes such as the Cortez, which had a middle sole of foam, a novelty at the time. Nike also carved out a niche for itself in Europe with its running shoes, as manufacturers tried to outdo one another, devising ever more ways to improve cushioning: shock absorbing techniques, based on either air or gel, became increasingly innovative. A countertrend has appeared in recent years, however, with sports doctors and runners questioning the point of too much padding, and classics from the not-so-distant past of running shoes have loomed back into public consciousness. Brütting's Roadrunner has a whole new circle of fans and some athletes have even rediscovered running barefoot on grass. But the main trend toward high-tech hasn't replaced the really important factors affecting performance—the running surface, the foot, and the sprinter's strength; too much technology can even be a hindrance rather than a help.

Modern running shoes such as these by adidas prioritize low weight and cushioning.

Equestrian Footwear

The history of the riding boot is more than just the history of footwear worn by amateur and professional riders in modern equestrian disciplines and sports—it involves a whole portrait gallery of boots. The horse riding fraternity can now buy dress, jump, and polo boots, as well as paddock boots and winter riding boots, all of which have their antecedents and predecessors. However, other types of ancient riding boot have long since fallen out of use, such as the knight's inner boot, which was worn under a suit of armor, and the top boot

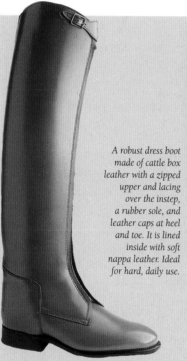

A robust dress boot made of cattle box leather with a zipped upper and lacing over the instep, a rubber sole, and leather caps at heel and toe. It is lined inside with soft nappa leather. Ideal for hard, daily use.

A polo boot in traditional brown. Black boots would discolor on impact with other players.

or heavy boot for a postilion riding the lead horse at the front of a coach. In the 18th century, there were also various sorts of gaiters and overshoes, so-called "stirrup shoes" or "stirrup boots," designed so they could be put on quickly and which also enabled riding in ordinary shoes and pants while protecting booted limbs. Modern riding boot shapes date back to the mid-16th century and are apparently based on designs imported from the Orient— riding boots have been known in Persia since the 14th century. The bucket tops common in the 16th and 17th century, which presumably were intended to protect the pants leg, were either fixed or could be folded over, but are no longer found on modern riding boots. Only the Spanish Riding School retains boots with a fixed top that are intended to protect the knee from injury. Otherwise, the basic form of the riding boot has changed

An all-round boot suitable for all aspects of riding. The zip fastening makes it easier to get on and off and the molded soles allow the wearer to negotiate rough terrain on foot. Popular for beginners or to keep in reserve as a spare pair.

A dress boot in classic black. It should give the rider as much support as possible, which is why the outer side of the upper extends a long way up the leg.

Ankle boots with elasticized side panels are a popular alternative to riding boots.

With its contrasting elastic, this boot looks more like a fashionable Chelsea boot.

Derby lacing molds the boot perfectly to the shape of the instep.

The Jodhpur boot is classic English equestrian sportswear and also looks good with jeans.

little: the ankle is supported by the construction of the upper, while the legging portion provides grip and protection for the lower leg. The sole should be able to slide in and out of the stirrup easily, and the heel is stiffened to force the foot into a position that enables the fitting of spurs and makes riding in the European style easier.

The shape of the boot depends upon the equestrian discipline. The dress boot is particularly long and features slightly thinner leather on its inner side. The heel cap extends some way up the leg and can be fitted with spurs. The boots are sometimes zipped to make them easier to get on.

Jump boots are a little softer, allowing more freedom of movement, and they often feature a decorative top of a differing color leather. Jump boots are also used for hunting and hacking and

Warm calves: ankle boots can withstand winter weather when worn with lambswool-lined gaiters, also known to riders as chaps.

A jump boot whose design is somewhat different from traditional models: light brown leather with a fabric panel on the inside combined with laces to allow the fit to be adjusted perfectly.

therefore the upper leather is stiffer to afford extra protection.

Polo boots have to protect the leg as well, although in this case more against stray balls, mallet blows, and the boots of other players, than thorns and branches. For this reason, they are made of especially strong or layered leather that is always colored brown; black boots would discolor on impact with other riders. Winter riding boots are also

available and even riding boots that are easy to walk in; players in the field are occasionally required to dismount and walk alongside their horses.

Paddock boots, either rubber-coated or in the form of Jodhpur boots, are another choice of footwear for horsemen and -women. They are worn with long riding pants and can be complemented with gaiters or chaps as required.

(All models supplied by A. Königs.)

Walking and

Someone who generally only travels by motorized transport may have trouble gauging distances to be walked on foot; after all, how long do a couple of miles take by car? Just a minute or so. Walking a couple of miles on foot can be delightful, or, at the end of a long trek, pure torture. Distances can only be comprehended in walking terms when they are actually covered on foot, which is why walking is an activity that everyone should try.

To prevent the walking experience from getting too human, all too human, however, the right footwear is recommended. The specialty manufacturers offer a wide range of shoes for different types of walking: there are shoes for strolling, for a long hike along marked paths on the flat, for gentle trips through the hills, for mountains, and for deserts. The exact dividing line between hiking and climbing boots is a movable feast and the differences are often hard to spot: they are related to the height of the shoe, the material used for the upper, and the composition of the sole. However, the ankle area is always protected, albeit to a greater or lesser degree, and the material

The plastic sole of this leather walking boot by Meindl provides cushioning on a range of terrains and the high profile of the upper helps to prevent twisted ankles.

Climbing Boots

used for the upper should provide stability and be breathable. The soles have to cushion each step and also provide protection against moisture and possible stones or shale. Hiking and climbing boots were made of leather before the invention of synthetic fabrics, and sewn manufacturing styles such as double-stitching were preferred to make them as stable as possible. Until the early 20th century, the soles were often made of leather reinforced with hobnails, although rubber soles with a molded pattern became popular from the 1930s. Rubber soles are more wear-resistant, better cushioned, and in particular provide more grip than leather soles. Different plastics are used nowadays, including polyurethane for glued shoes with injection-molded soles. Leather soles are only used for so-called "Haferl" shoes, whose construction and vamp styling identifies them as hiking shoes for mountainous terrain, although boots with leather soles are more the "Sunday driver" version of a walking boot than one designed for proper, vigorous usage.

The construction and materials of this mountain boot by HANWAG make it relatively lightweight, although it provides sufficient support for the foot. The rubber stone guard is typical.

Trekking, hiking, and mountaineering boots have to do a variety of jobs: they have to provide sufficient cushioning on flat ground and man-made paths, although the protection from stones or shale that is essential for mountain boots is not required of the lighter models. In both cases, traditionalists swear by double-stitched models with leather uppers, while modern variants are made from synthetic, but waterproof and breathable fabrics combined with leather.

BOOTS ARE MORE THAN SHOES, SOMETHING THAT IS TRUE IN MORE WAYS THAN ONE.

Boots

People think of boots as particularly masculine; boots are associated with fighting, manual labor, and cowboys, and were indeed invented to protect the legs for a variety of reasons. The first of these was probably the cold, and originally, boots for general wear were found throughout the more northerly regions of the world; elsewhere, boots such as waders, riding boots, or military jackboots were designed and reserved for particular purposes.

From the 17th century onward, however, boots were increasingly worn by the upper classes to be fashionable, and right into the 20th century it was entirely normal for gentlemen to wear ankle boots, the cut-down version of full-length boots, with morning or evening dress. The so-called "half-shoe" became increasingly popular from the 1920s and this term, which neatly describes how people saw this style at the time (i.e. not as a complete shoe), now refers to the standard shape of the formal lace-up.

With the exception of the Chelsea and chukka types, boots are not worn with a suit or pants and a sport coat anymore, and even these two exceptions only go with sporty suits and smart-casual combinations. Being confined to leisurewear, slip-on boots are also never seen with a dinner suit these days; boots worn for work are confined to the sturdy kind suitable for gardening and manual labor or construction work only. Work boots made by traditional American manufacturers are especially popular with fashion-conscious city-dwellers, as indeed are cowboy boots, whose fans can rarely actually ride a horse.

Boots are a type of footwear that more than any other expresses an attitude to life, or a kind of yearning or aspiration—wearing them is rarely prompted by any kind of necessity. Boots are really only justified in winter and someone wearing them at another time of year is either trying to break out of the straitjacket of convention, is seeking freedom and adventure, being particularly masculine (or trying to be), or is of a romantic or nostalgic bent.

Gum boots are as much a part of the clichéd image of smart rural life as are an English waxed jacket and waterproof boots—an almost essential requirement in the countryside on rainy days.

The Styles

Timberland's yellow boots are a much-copied classic, often worn by style- and status-conscious young people with a polo shirt and a waxed jacket. (Model: Timberland)

Lace-up styles are particularly popular with boot fans. You can wear pants over them, tuck the pants in, or even leave the boots unlaced if you really must. (Model: Red Wing)

Slip-on boots, such as the original style of motorcycle boots, have the advantage that they are quick to put on. Getting them off again may need the help of a boot jack, however. (Model: Red Wing)

Elasticized ankle boots are usually worn under pant legs, but many men choose to wear them with Bermuda shorts in summer. (Model: Tricker's)

The general resurgence of boots in recent years has kept the feet of many men warm over winter; full-length styles with a fur lining are especially snug. (Model: Meindl)

There is a long tradition of felt boots in Russia. They are a little less expensive as felt is cheaper than leather and they provide effective protection against the cold. (Model: Ludwig Reiter)

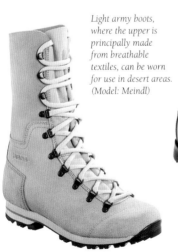

Light army boots, where the upper is principally made from breathable textiles, can be worn for use in desert areas. (Model: Meindl)

Welted boots with a lambswool lining can be worn with a sport coat and corduroys, and will even go with a sporty tweed suit. (Model: Prime Shoes)

Specialized Boots

Boots were developed in order to protect the legs—that the resulting footwear could also be considered attractive was simply an added bonus, but it has now become fashion's *raison d'être*. In the various activities where extra protection of the extremities is required, however, the focus is still on the purpose and functionality of boots.

Long before rubber and plastic were available, leather was the most important raw material used in the making of boots. Properly treated, it was relatively effective at keeping out water, and even leather soles

Chainsaw boots are often worn by people working in gardens or who need to saw wood with power tools, to feed a wood-burning stove, for example.

You don't need special boots to change a light bulb, but they are vital for workers maintaining high-voltage transmission towers.

could be made impervious to damp for a while through repeated tanning with oak bark. The seams were sealed against water penetration with tarred thread, but leather boots were very heavy and required considerable care to keep them in good order. By contrast, rubber and plastic boots are much lighter and require far less cleaning and care. Specialized boots are intended to provide protection against water, cold, heat, fire, acids, oil, and mechanical hazards, and are thus often equipped with special coatings, membranes, and reinforcement, such as steel inserts. Some boots worn for professional use are subject to strict controls and production requirements, in order to protect the health and safety of their wearers, although non-professionals buying them should also bear in mind the need for seeking out good quality and take note of the instructions for use.

Access to refineries and chemical production plants is only permitted in special boots that provide protection against oil and chemicals.

Firefighters wear fire- and heat-resistant boots; rubber would not be the best choice for their working conditions.

Gum Boots

The history of the gum boot begins in 1852, when Charles Goodyear, an American inventor, patented vulcanization, a method for transforming natural rubber into a robust work material. Goodyear began producing tires, while the patent for manufacturing footwear was acquired by Hiram Hutchinson, who founded a company in France, constructed a factory, and created the brand name "A L'Aigle," known today as AIGLE ("Eagle"). AIGLE is pretty much the French national gum boot.

The now legendary Bison model for gardening was introduced in 1968, the blue gum boot with white edging for sailors was launched in 1972, and the equestrian Ecuyer, which looks deceptively similar to a leather boot, hit the market in 1980.

The British version of the story ran in parallel to its colonial cousin: the American Henry Lee Norris had also developed a vulcanization process and his North British Rubber Company, founded in Edinburgh in 1857, was later to be renamed Hunter. By the end of the Second World War, the company had outgrown its original premises and production was moved to an old automobile plant in Dumfries, Scotland; built in 1908, the brick building is now a listed monument. The company launched a boot on the market for the 1954–5 winter

Green "wellies" are synonymous with the Sloane Ranger lifestyle; real country folk stick to black gum boots, which is why Prince Charles is happy to be snapped every now and again wearing just such a style. (Left) Light gum boots by Nokia, Finland: just the thing for a stroll by the lake.

Gum boots are sometimes made with a smooth sole studded with hobnails; this provides less grip but makes them easier to clean.

"hunter green." Today the company also makes accessories such as umbrellas.

Le Chameau, another French brand, was founded by Claude Chamot in Cherbourg in 1927, a little later than AIGLE and Hunter. Having manufactured top-quality boots for hunters and farmers from the outset, it was to become famous for the leather-lined Saint Hubert model that was launched in 1950. Hunter also had a style with a leather lining in its range, the welted Sovereign Hunter, which was supplied with a choice of hobnailed or molded soles. Good-quality gum boots involve considerable work by hand—they are built up in layers on a last from the inside out and are then vulcanized. Injection-molded plastic boots, while much cheaper, are made purely by machine. These are easy to recognize as the boots have clearly been made from a mold and can be identified by the seams between the quarter parts.

(Below) Hunter's top-of-the-range model is a welted rubber boot with a leather lining. (Right) Dry feet thanks to these classic, flexible boots made by Nokia.

season that was to revolutionize the image of footwear.

The boots were green and fitted just like a proper shoe. Gum boots had previously been made on the spacious side so they were easy to take off, but they hadn't been sufficiently comfortable to walk much further in than across a paddock and back; by contrast, the new boots were almost like a walking shoe and they transformed the image of rural footwear. Black boots were now worn only by "proper" country people, with well-off commuters to the City of London, for example, preferring green boots for hunting or pruning roses in their cottage gardens. By coincidence, the firm also took its new name from the shade of green used for the boots, which was listed as

A Gum Boot

A boot display in the old Hunter factory in Scotland, where gum boots were made by hand.

is Born

Handmade gum boots are built up in layers on a last. The outer sole is made first.

The quarter parts of the boot upper are laid onto the last while the rubber material is still soft.

The last (the shape that forms the boot) is on a rotating mount, allowing the worker easier access.

The rubber material is made slightly sticky by the warmth of the room, so any marks or scratches can be erased without problem.

A long strip of rubber seals the back of the boot, covering the edges of the upper sections.

The buckle that adjusts the width of the top edge of the upper is attached.

A Gum Boot

A pair of boots is made from start to finish by one worker. If these were welted shoes, the process would be called "bench-made."

Construction of the sole, which is also made from the inside out, only begins once the upper is complete.

The rubber material, which is still soft, is dried with heat to give it its final shape.

The elastic weave of the lining is pulled over the last like a stocking and any excess trimmed off.

The molded sole is attached to the finished boot from the bottom. Size and model are indicated with a sticker.

Just as with a bespoke shoe, the edge between the upper and the sole is sealed and decorated by hand with a roller.

is Born

Finished boots waiting on a rack to be packed into boxes and prepared for dispatch.

Ankle Boots: Short but Stylish

Boots are among men's favorite footwear, and ankle boots—the little brother of the top boot—are almost more popular still. They look good with casual outfits, but some styles can also be worn with a suit, or at least with a jacket and pants.

Colored detailing is especially important with ankle boots; Tricker's, a rather conservative English manufacturer known for its Royal Warrant to supply Prince Charles, has shown considerable imagination and daring in inventing new styles.

The smooth black Chelsea boot is a timeless classic from the Britain of the 1960s.

Old-fashioned slip-on boots can be given a highly modern feel with colored elastic.

A gentleman is likely to treat colored leather uppers with suspicion; green is just about acceptable.

Prince Charles is just one of the people to have worn desert boots with a crepe sole on trips to hot and dusty regions.

Brown suede chukka boots with leather soles are the "Chucks" of the gentleman with more traditional tastes.

The Jodhpur boot is intended as riding wear, but is also made on lasts designed for boots for pedestrian use.

This slightly more down-to-earth model intended for country use has been popular for a number of years with urban men more inclined to take fashion risks.

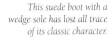

This suede boot with a wedge sole has lost all trace of its classic character.

The Cowboy Boot: a US Original

Classic men's fashion is rarely invented in a vacuum; the shape and form of garments and accessories are likely to be a result of customer demand and the craftsman's attempts to satisfy it. Hence, items of clothing or footwear have usually had many different contributors; the place and date of birth of the cowboy boot is certainly similarly obscure. Perhaps a particular shoemaker had some thoughts or ideas and shared them with a cattleman and so the boots took shape; however, if such a shoemaker ever existed, he remains anonymous. Nevertheless, cowboy boots are generally estimated to have been developed some time after 1865, when the American Civil War ended. A quick glance at a modern, colorfully decorated, luxury cowboy boot made from python leather reveals all the features you would expect of a typical model, but the first cowboy boots lacked decoration and were not made from exotic leather either.

Cowboy boots were primarily work boots and therefore as simple as you might expect—every design feature had a purpose. The extended uppers, which protected the leg from thorns, wire, and other hazards, were cut tightly enough for the boot to hold the calf securely but still with enough room to enable it to be shaken off in an emergency. The pointed toecap made it easier to slip into a stirrup and the heel anchored the foot to provide grip when controlling a horse with the legs and feet. Even the embroidered detailing on the outside has a purpose, as it stiffens the otherwise somewhat soft upper.

The first cowboy boots were individually commissioned from local craftsmen by cattle drovers; at the end of the 19th century, bespoke shoe- and bootmakers were as much the rule in rural areas of the USA as they were in Europe. This kind of footwear should not be thought of as a fine bespoke product in the modern sense of the word and certainly not as a luxury item; the lasts, probably just picked out of the craftsman's current stock and not necessarily custom-made, were fashioned by hand with as much skill as the maker could muster.

The Tony Lama brand has been making cowboy boots since 1911—all by hand and in the USA, as the website proudly proclaims.

By the end of the 19th century, boots were increasingly being stockpiled and sent out across the length and breadth of the USA by mail order; the big cities also had independent retailers that sold shoes, of course. Cowboy boots gained in popularity as a fashion item thanks to the Western movies, in which the heroes wore them as part of their cattleman costumes, and their fame spread across the USA.

But aside from in the movie theaters, Americans from the big cities on the east coast have about as much to do with cowboys and their boots as the bowler-hatted British businessman has with the sturdy boots of the traditional British "bobby" on the beat. Cowboy boots established themselves as a part of American culture between the 1930s and the 1950s, embodying raw masculinity, an affinity with nature, and a pioneering spirit. The movies also made the boots famous in Europe, although for years they were only very seldom available to buy there, not least since they were not suitable for the European style of riding.

The cowboy boot's epiphany as a fashion item came at the end of the 1970s, and during the great denim boom, teamed with Levi's 501s and a Chevignon shirt, they were popular as part of the smart-casual outfits of the 1980s. Cowboy boots have an aesthetic appeal for many men, but as they are not designed for covering long distances on foot, they are not really suitable as day shoes. This is not a problem in the USA, where people mainly use cars to get around, but their lack of comfort for walking is an obstacle to the popularity of cowboy boots in Europe.

Whether their favorite footwear is suitable for hiking or not is less of an issue for genuine cowboy boot fans, however—a real man can put up with a little discomfort. Devotees generally insist that their boot of choice is very comfortable, and this is determined by the method used in the manufacture. Despite their heels and pointed toes, good cowboy boots are welted and thus pleasant to wear—as long as they fit. Spanish manufacturers dominate the European market while the USA favors domestic products, although Mexican producers are also popular.

Snakeskin is often used for these boots as snakes are commonly found in the traditional home states of the cowboys.

Contrasting types of leather are typical of cowboy boots. The combination is sometimes the result of design considerations, sometimes an attempt to save on expensive leather.

Cowboy boots for use in stables are often fitted with specially resistant plastic soles.

It is of course every cowboy boot fan's dream to have a pair of their favorite footwear made to measure, and bespoke boots are considered an important status symbol by film stars, oil millionaires, country music performers, and rodeo artistes alike. A squad of established bespoke bootmakers meets this demand with creations handmade from the finest leather using traditional techniques. Such footwear masterpieces are too good for cattle-wrangling and so more down-to-earth styles are usually chosen for everyday use. To make them even more suitable for daily wear, they are often fitted with waterproof (and horse urine-proof!) plastic soles.

The pointed toecap of the boot may look uncomfortable, but this style of footwear was not designed for long walks.

The stitching on the upper of a cowboy boot was not originally for decoration, but was instead intended to stiffen the leather.

The heels of cowboy boots have developed from the style of horseback riding popular in the USA; the heel anchors the foot in the stirrup when you are in the saddle.

Questions

QUESTION: Can I wear smooth, black boots with a suit in the office?

ANSWER: Boots often seem too sporty or too rough-and-ready to go with a business suit. You wouldn't wear biker's boots with a pinstripe suit, of course, but the more discreet styles of ankle boots are theoretically fine; the modern half-shoe is just a cut-down low boot, although the style didn't emerge as a shoe in its own right until the beginning of the 20th century.

QUESTION: Some men leave their laces undone when wearing boots. Is this acceptable?

ANSWER: It's entirely acceptable as far as fashion is concerned, although there remains the question of how sensible or practical it is to go around with unlaced boots. There is a clear risk that you will trip over your laces or even lose a shoe. But who cares about that when you're trying to look "cool"?

QUESTION: Do rubber boots with leather linings breathe better than ordinary rubber boots?

ANSWER: No, the leather lining just makes the rubber boots a little warmer and they will feel more pleasant against the skin,

for a short while at least. You are, however, just faking the feel of a shoe made entirely of leather and to a certain extent the moisture is just being stored, as it were, in the leather lining. Sweat from your feet can't escape when you wear this style of boot and this is why sooner or later your feet will feel clammy.

QUESTION: Is it better to wear jeans over boots or tucked in?

ANSWER: The answer to this question depends on current fashions and personal taste. If you wear boots over your jeans, they can be seen much more easily; worn under jeans, boots could just as easily be half-shoes or ankle boots.

QUESTION: Do cowboy boots look common?

ANSWER: The impression made by cowboy boots depends on their quality and also of course on the design. Authentic examples, such as those made by good manufacturers in the USA, Mexico, or Spain, might seem a little out of place in Europe but they should not be rejected out of hand. There is always the question, however, of where you can wear cowboy boots in earnest, outside their home territory of the USA. They are not designed for long walks

& Answers

and other boots are more usual for riding non-American style. With the exception of certain subcultures, cowboy boots will thus always be the preserve of eccentrics who often seem to find them comfortable despite their pointed shape; this may be a result of their welted construction and the footbed this creates.

QUESTION: I always find it difficult to get my boots off. What should I do?

ANSWER: Boot wearers should definitely invest in a boot jack. This is not a domestic servant, but a wooden or plastic tool that helps with the removal of boots. You should avoid bracing your boots against a step to remove them as this can damage the leather of the heel.

QUESTION: I think Jodhpur boots are smart. Are they suitable for everyday wear?

ANSWER: Every style of riding boot of European provenance has a relatively stiff outer sole, which is useful in the saddle but not much good for walking. For this reason, riding boots of all kinds are not especially comfortable for walking any distance. As Jodhpur boots have long since been discovered as leisurewear, however, most manufacturers offer them as welted shoes with a sole suitable for walking.

QUESTION: When wearing a suit to work, I regularly get cold feet on the bus or train in winter. What can I do?

ANSWER: If your office has a strict dress code and you have even the slightest notion of what constitutes an appropriate outfit, heavy winter boots with a suit are right out. You might have to resort to galoshes; these protect the shoe and provide a little warmth if you go for an ankle-height model. Just take off the galoshes with your coat at the office. Alternatively, wear warm boots on the way to work and then change into classic leather-soled lace-ups at the office. There are also ankle boots with a lambswool lining and rubber soles that have a slim profile and could be worn with a dark tweed suit, but they would usually be too warm in a heated workspace. The upshot is that it would be best to change shoes on arrival.

QUESTION: Are gaiters still a viable alternative to boots these days?

ANSWER: There are calf-length gaiters that can replace long top boots. Up to the 1930s, short, felt "spats," usually gray in color, were worn with half-shoes. These ankle-high gaiters kept the feet warm up to a point, but now look outdated and old-fashioned. A classic, laced boot is probably a better choice; with its toecap, it will look like an Oxford or brogue under your pants.

CORRECT CARE EXTENDS THE LIFE OF THE SHOE AND CAN EVEN HELP CALM FRAZZLED NERVES.

Care and Cleaning

Some men find the task of cleaning shoes relaxing—instead of strolling in the woods or mowing the lawn, they prefer to polish leather. They may even make a pleasant evening of it over a glass of wine with some other shoe enthusiasts, sprucing up their often extremely expensive lace-ups and bringing them up to a mirror shine. Others will let their shoes rot away almost to nothing before reaching for the cleaning brushes. Those in the anticleaning camp will have a variety of reasons for being disinclined to look after their footwear—some men are just too lazy, others have never been taught the point or use of clean shoes, others again wear shoes that don't really need too much care and attention, while some are even said to regard polished shoes as highly suspect. But it is likely that if you are reading this book, you are strongly in favor of cleaning shoes, even if it would sometimes be nicer if the work could be left to a shoeshine boy or a manservant.

There is a distinction in shoe care between the cleaning intended to extend the lifespan of the shoe or improve its functionality, and the cleaning that is an end in itself, designed to produce a pair of beautiful shiny shoes. The difference is simple: if the objective is to merely look after a pair of shoes, they can be kept supple with a polish or cream that will make the material of the upper waterproof. But if the wearer continues polishing until a brilliant shine is produced, they are either obeying an aesthetic impulse or are conforming to peer pressure.

As many people have nothing to gain from shiny shoes and the public no longer expects perfectly polished shoes at school, work, or in a restaurant, shiny shoes that are well looked after have become something of a rarity. Readers whose schooldays date back to the 1980s may still have come across teachers who would reprimand pupils for their unpolished shoes—as a joke, of course, but even so. This is certainly no longer the case, and while that is no loss, it is still necessary to stand up for shoe care if you are interested in extending the useful life of your footwear as far as possible.

A turpentine wax polish, a cotton cloth, and a polishing brush—the basic kit for looking after smooth leather shoes is not extensive and needn't cost the earth. (Photo: Eduard Meier)

Polishing Events

More and more shoe stores and gentlemen's outfitters are offering their customers so-called "shoe-cleaning seminars." The demonstrator reveals the best ways of cleaning shoes of different kinds of leather and answers questions about care products and footwear in general. Beer, wine—sometimes even champagne—and perhaps a little bite to eat are served, either during the demonstration or afterward, making the evening even more agreeable.

Eduard Meier's shoe store in Munich offers training sessions such as these, which are usually conducted by Peter Eduard Meier in person. The shoe and luxury clothing business that he runs with his sister has achieved a renown that has spread far beyond the Bavarian capital, and the pair now design the whole of the shoe, fabric, and accessory collections, look after the marketing and PR, train the staff, and sometimes even serve customers in the shop. Peter Eduard Meier's shoe seminars introduce participants to the secrets of high-shine polishing with water and how to wash shoes. Both techniques are very effective, but very few men are aware of them before taking part in the seminar.

Wax polish and water make for a perfect shine.

Technique improves with every new pair polished.

Depending on the polish, the shoe may retain its color or darken slightly.

(Left and below) Men can relax over wax polish and a glass of wine at a shoe-cleaning seminar.

Peter Eduard Meier is a past master in the art of shoe-cleaning.

The Basics: Looking After Your Shoes

Shoe care begins long before you take out the brushes and polish—it starts with the use of a shoehorn. Shoe trees also play an important role, if you bear in mind that that shoe care involves much more than just producing a superficial shine, a practice which in any case should not be denounced as mere vanity: smooth, polished leather repels liquids and the layer of wax that creates the perfect shine also functions as a barrier against dirt.

1 Most people think of polishing when they think of shoe care. Dust, dirt, and anything else sticking to the leather of the upper should first be removed. You can happily use water for this, either with a dampened brush, a moist cloth, or indeed directly under running water. Dried-on soil residue, tiny stones, and a mixture of dust, tire debris, and oil can usually be rinsed out of molded soles; more stubborn dirt can also be worked out with a small wooden stick (not too sharp) or a toothbrush. This first phase of cleaning is often neglected and instead a thick layer of polish is slapped on to leather that is still dusty. If this happens once in a while, it will not harm the shoe, but as a rule, as much dust as possible should be removed from the shoe. before polishing

TIP: With shoes made from soft leather, such as expensive sneakers, you should be careful about using water. In such cases, remove dust with a gently moistened cloth and a very soft brush. A soft or medium brush should be used to remove dust from synthetic fabrics, such as those used for the uppers of sneakers. A vacuum cleaner with a brush fitting can also be very useful, but remember to turn the suction down to a low setting.

2 A lot of men would hesitate to use water for cleaning their shoes. This is understandable; you would generally assume that leather and water do not mix well, and there is some truth to this. No one would recommend walking for hours in the rain in leather shoes, not because the shoes will get damaged, but rather because your feet will get wet. As long as the shoes have a chance to dry

out, water need not be regarded as the enemy, and leather shoes can withstand the occasional dip. Total immersion is, however, not usually recommended; it is also not required for normal care. After washing, shoes must of course be allowed to dry completely and should be stuffed with newspaper and left to dry in a warm, well-ventilated room. This process should not be hurried, which means not putting the shoes in front of a heat source and certainly not using a hairdryer or an oven for speedier drying.

The penny loafer from SEBAGO (left) and the Oxford from Crockett & Jones are essential classic shoes.

3 After cleaning the uppers, the next step is to apply some grease, in the form of wax polish or cream, for example. Using a little brush like a toothbrush will help you to get into the corners, such as between the welt and the upper. The grease is intended to make the leather supple and water-resistant. It stops water from getting in and prevents cracks and tears. The final polishing initially removes any cream or polish residue and ultimately prevents your clothes from getting dirty or smeared. Black wax polish can leave marks on the pants seam of light suits that are almost impossible to get off. Polishing also makes sure that moisture is repelled and dirt cannot stick quite so easily.

TIP: There is also an aesthetic side to a mirror shine, and those who are able to appreciate this will be delighted by the sight of leather with a luster reminiscent of the patina on old furniture. Men who reduce shoe care to merely producing a shiny surface have not grasped the proper meaning of the process, and quick-shine products are not recommended for this reason. Other than producing a fine shine, they are good for very little else and may even cause harm to the leather in the long run.

4 Fabric shoes such as canvas sneakers are never polished. Instead, care begins and ends with washing and brushing, or rubbing dirt from the uppers. A treatment spray takes over the protective function of the polish. Keeping a white shoe white has little to do with care and much more to do with appearance, as it is a cosmetic procedure only. Whether you are of the school of thought that a little dirt on a white shoe merely creates an interesting patina, or whether you find it unattractive, is naturally a question of taste and for what purpose the shoe is to be worn; gleaming white shoes are, of course, essential when part of a uniform.

The Basics:

The shoe is first cleaned with a brush and a damp cloth to remove dust and dirt.

A good polish, such as Burgol from Switzerland, is applied to every part and allowed to soak in.

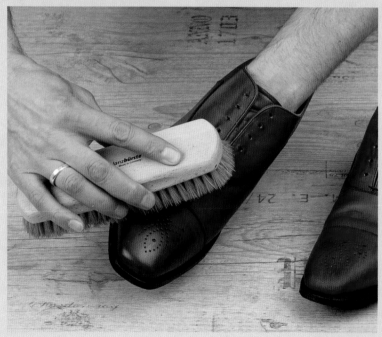

After the polish has soaked in, it is buffed with a natural-bristle brush. If the shoes have been polished regularly, they are now ready.

Wax Polish

New shoes should be re-treated with wax polish after the first going-over, and here you can use a soft cloth.

After allowing the polish to soak in, the shoes should be polished again for the final time.

Basic care of shoes protects the leather and creates a lasting shine.

Tips for Extending

1 **USE A SHOEHORN** You should always have a shoehorn to hand when taking off or putting on your shoes. Always pack one when going away, as not every hotel will provide one. If there is no shoehorn available, place a cloth or a sock in the back of the heel and allow your foot to slide over it into the shoe. Alternatively, you might be able to use a flexible piece of card. Always undo the laces before removing your shoes or the leather will wear out on the instep and the shoe will eventually become too loose.

2 **NO STICK-ON SOLES** Some shoe retailers advise their customers to have a thin layer of rubber stuck to their soles, which is intended to protect them and make them waterproof. Manufacturers are not keen on this idea as the additional layer stiffens the leather sole, the shoe cannot bend properly when the foot is moving, and the full weight of the body is borne by the leather of the upper. If you spend a lot of time walking wet streets, buy a shoe with a rubber sole—welted shoes do not necessarily have to have leather soles.

3 **AVOID LONG-TERM USE** Wear each pair of shoes for one day and then let them rest for a day. If you sweat heavily, give them two days' rest. If you have been wearing them for a long time, for example on a business trip, they will need several days of rest in a well-ventilated room. Only a completely dry shoe is comfortable.

4 **ON WITH THE SHOE TREES** After removing your footwear, place shoe trees in the still-warm shoes and adjust them to fit; this will stop creases made by the action of walking from forming in the leather. If you would prefer to avoid taking heavy wooden shoe trees on a trip, use lighter plastic ones instead.

5 **DO NOT FORGET TO CLEAN YOUR SHOES** Cleaning your shoes every so often is vital. If you alternate two pairs of shoes in the office, for example, you should clean each pair roughly every two weeks. This makes them water-resistant and keeps the leather supple, and anyway, dirty shoes look a bit sloppy.

6 **ALLOW AIR TO GET TO THE SOLES** Wet shoes? Stuff them with newspaper immediately. If they are only a bit damp, shoe trees will do. Shoes should in any case be placed on their sides to dry so the moisture can escape from the soles more easily; otherwise, the undersides of the shoes may not dry properly, especially on tiled, laminate, or PVC floors, and will still be

the Life of Your Shoes

clammy the next day. And as has been mentioned elsewhere, never try to speed up drying with a hairdryer or an artificial heat source.

7 A STITCH IN TIME Check heel rubbers regularly. They should be renewed before the leather shows through. The outer sole must be replaced and/or repaired before a hole can develop. For glued or through-stitched shoes, a new layer of leather is applied.

Important note: make sure expensive shoes and welted models are only repaired by someone with the necessary expertise, which is generally not on offer in the express heel bar at a shopping mall or DIY center. Many shoe manufacturers offer a repair service whereby the shoes are mounted on their original lasts and replaced with original materials. You can usually get information about this service from shoe retailers or directly from the factory.

Everything You Need

Polishing brushes with natural bristles.

*Polishes and creams
for shoe care.*

*Leather polish
and a range of suede
care products.*

for Shoe Care

The right color for every leather.

Cream for softer kinds of leather.

Professional products: leather sole oil and shoe cleaner.

Care for delicate shoes.

Special brush for suede leather shoes.

Shoe Trees

The owner of Eduard Meier, a traditional Munich shoe retailer founded in 1596 and now run by the 13th generation of the family, regards shoe trees as the most important item in shoe care. This may initially sound strange coming from a man who sells a wide range of expensive shoe care products, but there is much truth in it. In an ideal world, a shoe tree should fit a shoe as well as the last on which the shoe was made, thus enabling the tree to return the shoe to its original shape. This is of crucial importance to retaining the shoe's appearance and function.

Shoe trees are made of a range of materials and in a variety of shapes. The simplest types are made of plastic and metal, the most expensive variety are made of wood and fill the shoe completely. Simple shoe trees are nonetheless good for stretching the shoe a little after wear and preventing them from bending upward over time. Deep creases in the uppers, where the leather can start to press down on the foot or even crack, are also prevented. The better kinds of shoe trees, similar in appearance to the last or even carved as an exact copy, return the shoe even more exactly to shape: bespoke shoemakers generally supply such perfectly formed shoe trees and they are sometimes available for off-the-shelf shoes as well.

Dinckelacker also supplies made-to-measure shoe trees for bespoke shoes.

Shoe experts are still in two minds as to whether the shoe tree should be varnished or made from untreated wood. This is to do with whether the shoe tree should be able to absorb the moisture that has been transferred to the leather during wear. One camp maintains that only untreated wood can absorb moisture while the other believes that this is not the shoe tree's job and prefer the varnished variety.

If you follow through on the idea that a shoe tree should absorb moisture, you reach a somewhat strange conclusion: just like the shoe itself, the tree would have to rest for a while after use in order to dry out. Proponents of the theory that unvarnished shoe trees are better should try them out. There is some doubt surrounding the theory and no real evidence that shoe trees do indeed absorb moisture, yet the insides of shoes placed on varnished shoe trees are usually completely dry after a couple of days.

Inserting a shoe tree is simple—the front end is placed into the tip of the shoe and the other end into the heel. Models with a screw action must first be extended to exert enough pressure. But be careful: too much pressure can be bad for the shoe. If a lot of pressure is required to force the shoe tree into the shoe, the tree is too tight. The sole should be straight or even slightly concave. Slip-on shoes, which bend more as the foot moves in walking, can stand slightly tighter shoe trees than lace-ups.

(Below) An exact fit is important for a shoe tree. (Photo: Eduard Meier)

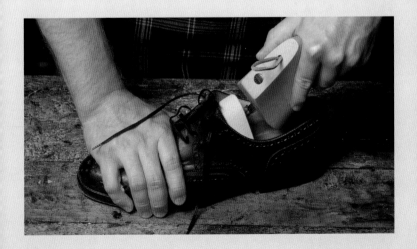

Storing Shoes

If you only have a handful of pairs of shoes to call your own, you will have no problems storing or transporting them. They will fit in a wardrobe or under a cupboard, or in some other place in the house, but there are plenty of men who, whether they are sneaker wearers or fans of upmarket welted shoes, own considerably more than two pairs. If space is not an issue, they can be stored on shelves; the best shelves have racks or mesh for the shoes to rest on, allowing air to circulate around the soles. Shelves in closed cupboards stop the shoes from getting too dusty, but the enclosed environment is not good for ventilation. Shoes that are worn only rarely can therefore be stored in bags or in their original boxes. Shoes stored on a shelf but only worn infrequently will need to be dusted occasionally and a feather duster, for example, is perfect for this job.

When you are traveling, a single pair of shoes is reasonably easy to carry in

Bags provide protection from dust and prevent marks from getting on the clothes in your case.

A shoe box for the shelf by Shoepassion.

hand luggage. Shoe bags are usually supplied with good-quality shoes, making it easy to stow them in a travel bag or suitcase. Wooden shoe trees are usually rather heavy (depending on shoe size), so light plastic ones are generally recommended, or shoes can be stuffed with clean socks on the way out and dirty ones on the way back. If the overall weight of luggage is not an issue—such as when traveling by car, for example—shoe trees can be left in the shoes. For lovers of tradition, or those with a taste for luxury, a special suitcase with suitable subdivisions may be purchased; in the days when the wealthy would travel with trunks containing a wardrobe for all occasions, a shoe case was standard issue and they are still available from some manufacturers. Shoe bags for sportsmen such as horseback riders are better value for money; they don't look quite so good, but they do the same job. Sneakers and leisure shoes such as deck shoes are easily stowed in a travel bag, but should also be stuffed with something so they don't get squashed.

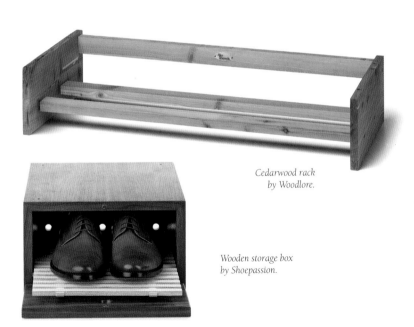

Cedarwood rack by Woodlore.

Wooden storage box by Shoepassion.

Polishing with Water

In Paris, a group of elegant French gentlemen regularly congregate as a kind of club to clean their shoes. Of course, rather than using regular finishing products, they polish their welted shoes with champagne. It's a nice story but probably a complete waste of fine bubbles, as you can achieve a mirror shine with water just as well.

Polishing with water is considered king among the various methods of cleaning goods made of smooth leather; most people who have had a little to do with leather shoes will have come across it at some stage, although very few use this technique on a regular basis. With a little extra time and effort, however, it can produce much better results than the usual method.

Before polishing, dust and dirt must first be removed from the shoe. Wax polish is then applied with a cloth to the edge of the soles, the welt, and the upper.

The polish should be applied sparingly. The following step differs from the usual wax polishing method. The part of the cloth where the polish has soaked in is dipped in water and you begin to rub the leather with a circular motion, starting with the largest area first. It is often recommended to let the shoe stand for a few hours after applying the wax polish. However, it is usually better to start polishing with water straight away, as some turpentine waxes can dry on the leather stubbornly and more water is required to polish them to a shine. Polishing with water works because the water

and wax repel each other. If you polish a shoe with a dry cloth, you are just taking away the residue of the previously applied polish that has not been absorbed. The damp cloth prevents this from happening and creates a thin film of wax between the cloth and the leather. The more often a smooth leather shoe is polished in this way, the quicker the process is completed.

1. Apply the turpentine wax. 2. Moisten the application cloth with water and polish. 3. Buff the leather. 4. The result: a beautiful mirror-like shine.

Galoshes

Until a few years ago, people wearing galoshes were the exception rather than the rule and anyone walking the streets wearing even black rubber overshoes would attract looks of amazement. Colorful galoshes were then launched on the market and became a hit, not so much with the general public, but particularly with wearers of welted shoes. The notion of marketing protective covers, which had once always been black, in a range of bright shades attracted both new customers and fans of classic fashion. They were now able to satisfy their desire for crazy colors with these shoe protectors, rather than with colorful suspenders, pants, or the lining of jackets, as they had done previously.

Galoshes originally sprang from the need to protect delicate shoes from the wet and, to a certain degree, the desire to spare the foot from the cold. The soles of galoshes also offer a better nonslip surface than leather soles. The idea of putting one shoe on top of another is a very old one. It was technically impossible to make an overshoe that was really waterproof until the 19th century; they were generally made of leather and the seams had to be caulked, with a varying degree of success. From the 19th century until around the time of the Second World War, galoshes, a raincoat, and an umbrella were important accessories found in many a home.

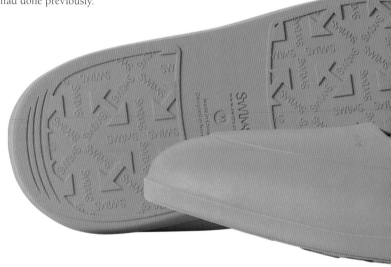

However, galoshes rely on the idea that shoes have great intrinsic value and are themselves worth protecting; someone who wears sneakers that they prefer to look as worn-out as possible has no need for overshoes. In addition to traditional rubber galoshes, which nowadays are not as a rule made from natural rubber, overshoes with uppers made from synthetic materials and a separate plastic sole are also available. From the outside, they look more like boots and their appearance, along with their light weight, makes them a good match for the generally casual styles of clothing favored by most people today.

Galoshes were the only really effective protection for shoes; they saved on the purchase of rainproof shoes for the winter, offered good value for money and lasted for a long time.

Available in a range of sometimes quite striking colors, these overshoes by SWIMS are like a smart raincoat for the good-quality shoe and even have a decorative sole.

How to Clean Suede Properly

Suede leather has unjustifiably acquired the image of being delicate or difficult to look after, but suede is only delicate in the respect that drops of water are immediately noticeable on light leather. They will not harm the leather and the amount of care required is minimal, particularly since with suede you are spared all that time-consuming polishing.

What we call suede includes a range of different kinds of leathers whose surface seems unfinished and feels velvety to the touch. This look and feel is achieved by napping the leather. If it is sanded on

Suede shoes usually get soiled by dust and dirt sticking to the surface.

First, the laces are removed so that every part of the shoe is accessible.

Special suede care products freshen up the color. It has to match the leather exactly, of course.

Using a soft brush, the suede product is worked in everywhere so that no part is overlooked.

the hair side, it is called nubuck; when sanded on the flesh side, it is known as velour leather. For top-quality men's shoes, the leather used is generally from cattle.

Care of suede leather involves removing dirt and then restoring and/or rearranging the structure of the fibers. Suede is not treated with polish but is waterproofed using a spray-on product. Dirt is removed mechanically through brushing down with a specialized suede leather brush, which may have rubber or metallic wire bristles. More stubborn stains are removed with leather erasers.

If the leather has been rubbed flat in areas of particular wear, it can be roughed up again using the brush. The color can be refreshed with a spray.

Suede leather shoes can be immersed in water too and if the shoe is soaked completely, there will be no lines when it dries. A bath will do the leather good if the shoe has got very dusty, but it is not a process that should be repeated too often. If you wish to clean a suede shoe quickly, you can just rub it down with a damp towel; this will remove some of the dust and straighten the leather fibers.

The dirt is removed with a suede leather brush. Stubborn dirt can be removed with a wire brush.

Engrained dirt can be removed with a leather eraser and the worn spot roughened up again.

Spray on the protective product. This will repel water and prevent dirt from sticking.

Replace the laces. The care required for suede leather shoes is minimal.

Repair and Maintenance

Up until really quite recently, shoes were extremely valuable possessions and so were looked after carefully and repaired repeatedly. The great majority of shoes

sold nowadays are cheap, disposable items that are not worth repairing, and repair is often not even possible. Sneakers especially, generally made from several different synthetic parts, tend to be extremely hard to mend, not least since the cobbler is unable to obtain original replacement parts for the uppers and soles, and a repair would disfigure the shoe.

As a rule, leather shoes are easy to repair. The top (the upper, with its vamp and quarter panels) is rarely badly damaged; cracks do occasionally appear across the upper and these can be stitched or patched in theory, although the repair is not likely to hold with very thin kinds of leather where the upper is very worn. Signs of wear are more common on the inside of the shoe: the lining at the heel or inside the toe can wear out, for example. This is not a problem to repair and it is worth doing, as a damaged heel can quickly destroy your socks. Be careful when repairing the lining at the front of the shoe; seams can protrude and press on the foot.

Most shoe repairs are confined to the soles and the heels, but to avoid the need to repair them, some people attach metal plates to the tips of the soles or the heels.

This was very much the fashion in the late 1980s, when it was championed by the fashion media. There can be no objection to metal plates at the toe, as they do indeed save on repairs, but plates on the heels are not recommended as they have no cushioning effect and every step taken is therefore felt directly in the back. Metal tips on heels are also extremely slippery. If you wear through rubber heels very quickly, you will just have to resign yourself to going to the mender's more often.

If the soles are worn through, there are two ways to repair them. For shoes with glued-on or through-stitched outer soles, the damaged sole is torn or sanded off and a suitable piece of sole leather is stuck on. It is also possible to attach a rubber sole as a replacement, of course.

With welted shoes, there is always the question of how much money should be spent on the repair. The most expensive option is to send the shoe back to the manufacturer (generally via a retailer) to be repaired with original parts. This is the best option for many shoe enthusiasts as they trust the manufacturer to restore the shoe to its original condition.

It can take several weeks for the shoe to come back, however. Alternatively, the sole can be replaced at a local shoe mender's, but it's advisable not to go to the first one you come across, as they often lack a feel for top-quality shoes and many repairers have no experience of the machinery and sole material required. Welted shoe specialists, however, are able to stitch the sole to the welt either by hand or with a machine. They can

also renew the welt or exchange the cork lining and often have access to original heel tips sourced from the various manufacturers.

Shoes restored in the Allen Edmonds factory in the USA look like new by the end of the process; only the patina is retained.

The Finest Repairs

Someone with only a fleeting interest in shoes might think of a shoemaker as someone who only repairs shoes, but a shoemaker can operate in a wide range of different specialist areas. Some do indeed make shoes and there are others who also repair them, but in many countries these are not only two different processes but also two different professions. The quality of a repair is likely to be much more satisfactory if the craftsman carrying out the work can also make shoes. Welted shoes are therefore generally repaired by companies that employ at least one

A welted shoe is resoled. First, the rubber heels are removed.

The outer sole is removed if the new leather sole is to be glued on.

The sole is taken back so that the shoes can be rebuilt from underneath.

The shoe without outer soles. You can see the old cork lining under the inner sole.

shoemaker or are run by a master craftsman in the field.

A shoe repair workshop deals mostly with outer soles and heels that have worn through, but it must also be able to repair uppers, both inside and out. Typical areas needing repair include the lining inside the heels that have worn through, inner linings with holes, cracks or holes in the uppers, or seams that have come undone. Only specialized workshops have the spare parts in stock and the machinery required for these jobs, let alone suitably qualified staff; in the case of high-quality welted shoes, the repairer often has to do the work by hand to ensure the shoe is restored to its original state.

The threads holding the outer sole to the welt are cut with a knife.

Once the threads are cut, the sole is removed with pliers.

The outline of the new outer sole is traced out on top-quality, vegetable-tanned sole leather.

The cobbler cuts out the rough shape of the sole around the traced outline.

The outer soles are glued on using a press, as they were at the manufacturer's. An overlap is initially left in place.

A machine cuts a narrow channel in the outer sole. The needle will pass through this when stitching the soles.

The natural color of the leather soles is stained to match the shoe. The ingredients for the dye are a secret.

The heels are often original replacement parts from the manufacturer or are made to match in the workshop.

The craftsman inspects the heels: a pair of shoes have to match exactly when viewed from underneath.

The heel is dyed to match the color of the outer soles. The "secret dye" is used here again.

Repairs

A genuine Goodyear sewing machine is used to attach the leather outer sole to the welt with canvas thread.

The seam does not continue right to the heel; only a few manufacturers continue the seam right around the shoe.

The heels are first glued to the outer sole under high pressure. A special press is used here too.

Then the heel is attached with nails. A heel is nailed on from the inside; this will later be covered with padding.

The heels and outer sole of the shoe, which has been reconstructed from the bottom up, are polished to a mirror-like shine on a machine.

A shoe repaired at "Schuh Konzept" in Berlin is restored to exactly the same condition as a new sample of the brand.

Shoehorns

In addition to shoe trees and polishing brushes, the shoehorn is the last of the three most important tools used in the care of leather shoes. The laces must first be loosened and then the foot can be slipped in effortlessly with the aid of a shoehorn. Never try to put on a shoe without a shoehorn; if there is not one to hand, a handkerchief or a flexible piece of card can be used. Putting your foot in the shoe directly places strain on the shoe's heel and in time it can become bent over. It is also uncomfortable for the heel of your foot.

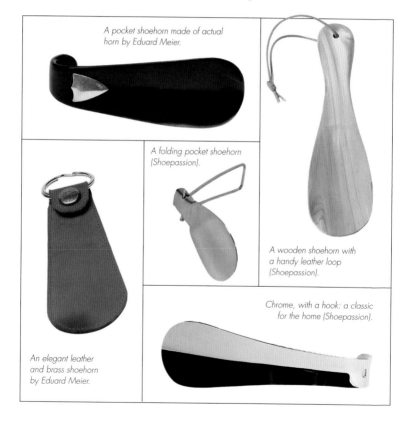

A pocket shoehorn made of actual horn by Eduard Meier.

A folding pocket shoehorn (Shoepassion).

A wooden shoehorn with a handy leather loop (Shoepassion).

Chrome, with a hook: a classic for the home (Shoepassion).

An elegant leather and brass shoehorn by Eduard Meier.

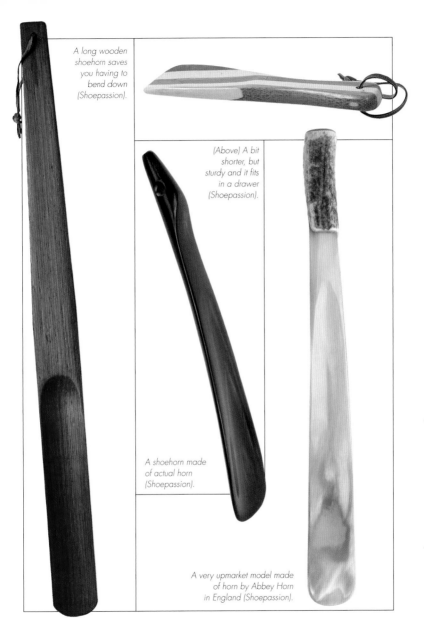

A long wooden shoehorn saves you having to bend down (Shoepassion).

(Above) A bit shorter, but sturdy and it fits in a drawer (Shoepassion).

A shoehorn made of actual horn (Shoepassion).

A very upmarket model made of horn by Abbey Horn in England (Shoepassion).

Care and Cleaning | 203

Questions

QUESTION: Should I have rubber soles glued to my leather soles?

ANSWER: Some shoe retailers advise their customers to stick a thin layer of rubber over their new leather soles to prevent the leather from sucking up water. Rubber soles also provide better grip. There is no reason to advise against this for shoes with glued or through-stitched soles, but it is better avoided in the case of welted shoes. Even a very thin rubber sole changes the way the shoe moves during walking; it becomes slightly less flexible and more of the body's energy is therefore transmitted to the leather of the upper, so it is subjected to more stress. Rubber soles have another disadvantage: factories will no longer accept the shoe for resoling, although of course this is in theory no longer necessary because of the rubber sole. It is ultimately also an aesthetic question: are you willing to disfigure your leather sole with a rubber sole or perhaps this is not an important consideration?

QUESTION: What do you think of quick-shine treatments?

ANSWER: Not much, as they dry out the leather and can make it fragile over time. It is better to clean shoes regularly. And if you would rather not do that, you might find a shoeshine service in your town.

QUESTION: How do you recommend dealing with snow stains?

ANSWER: There are a few folk remedies, but not all of them work. It is better to use dedicated products (available from specialists or on the Internet). The best solution, however, is to avoid snow stains in the first place, although this may be stating the obvious. Leather shoes can be well protected with galoshes or something similar, and it's also best to avoid stepping straight into a mound of snow by the side of the road. Spray-on products can also be effective at preventing snow stains.

QUESTION: What can I do about scratches in leather?

ANSWER: Superficial scratches can be removed with wax polish. Larger scrapes can be mended with repair paste. This works like a filler and once dried, the shoe is treated with a dye to match the shoe so that the repair is hardly visible. Deep scratches should be removed by an expert who will fill the hole in the leather with a hard wax; you can also do this yourself and the material required is available on the Internet. Scratches in leather footwear worn for equestrian sports are removed with polish and a "shoe bone": the scratch is layered with wax polish which is carefully worked into the leather with the bone.

& Answers

QUESTION: What is the quickest way to dry soaking wet shoes?

ANSWER: There is no quick way, at least not if you wish to avoid the shoes being damaged. Please do not use a hairdryer to dry them, or place them on the radiator or in the oven (as people are always doing). Hot air dries out the leather and makes it fragile. Instead, stuff the shoes with newspaper and leave them in a well-ventilated, moderately heated room. Replace with new paper every couple of hours until the shoes are finally dry, then insert some shoe trees and leave them to stand for a day. The water will not damage the shoes at all but drying takes time. This is why you should protect shoes with galoshes in wet weather or at least wear shoes with plastic soles.

QUESTION: How and with what do I clean patent leather shoes?

ANSWER: The leather of patent shoes has been completely covered with a gloss coating, so when cleaning them you are only treating the shiny surface, not the leather; special patent leather care products are available. To avoid cracks caused by repeated use, patent shoes should be put on shoe trees as soon as they are removed. Scratches and tears cannot be repaired, you just have to treat them as part of the patina.

QUESTION: What do I do when the leather lacing breaks on my deck shoes?

ANSWER: Leather lacing can be replaced and a specialist shop can sell you a special large needle with which the laces can be inserted, starting at the heel.

QUESTION: I have read that some people polish their shoes with champagne. Does this achieve anything?

ANSWER: If it achieves anything at all, it is due to the mixture of carbon dioxide and alcohol. Anyone wishing to try it should use cheap cava—champagne is far too good for an experiment like this. Otherwise water is fine as well—how to achieve a high-gloss polish is described earlier in this chapter.

QUESTION: What do I do if I forget my shoehorn on a trip?

ANSWER: Open lace-up shoes as wide as possible and then slide the foot carefully in. For slip-ons, place a cloth (such as a silk handkerchief) in the heel and let the foot slip in over that. A small, flexible piece of card can also be used as a replacement shoehorn.

Etiquette and Styling

Which shoes should you choose? There is such a wide range of footwear on the mar¬ket that you may find making a choice difficult. When faced with so many different styles, if you are not sure of exactly what you want when shopping for shoes, you might begin to feel confused. A classic model for business, deck shoes for smart–casual occasions, sneakers for leisurewear, whichever style of flip-flop or sandal is in fashion for hot weather, something extravagant in black for the evening, or will an all-round shoe be a better option? Practical, comfortable, easy-care, and cheap to boot?

Which shoe you go for is not just a matter of personal taste or fashion; dress codes often need to be taken into consideration too. Bank staff are generally expected to wear conservative outfits, for example, and black shoes are part of this as a rule. If you are earning your living as an assistant in a sneakers store, however, you would look a little out of place with highly polished lace-ups. Equally, brown or light-colored shoes would not be right for a funeral. However, not everyone has to, or indeed wishes to, choose shoes according to prevailing fashions or dress code rules; many men are prompted to make their selection only by their personal preferences.

In all cases, however, knowingly or not, people are expressing something with their shoes, even if it is just that their footwear is revealing their disregard for conven-tion or complete lack of interest in aesthetics. As clothes say, or even betray, a lot about us, it is worth everyone's while to choose shoes with care. People who think about how they combine their clothes to make an outfit will also choose their shoes with care.

Shoes are rightly thought of as the foundation of a look; they round off your gen-eral appearance and often provide the finishing touch. A good suit only really looks good when the shoes match, but it is not just suit-wearers who know how important shoes are—a lot of young people would not leave the house without the right sneak-ers, someone who loves the great outdoors will wear the latest activity footwear what-ever the season, and a biker wouldn't be seen dead wearing Birkenstock sandals as he mounts his Harley.

Interest in footwear has kept pace with men's growing awareness of good styling, whether for business or a smart leisure look.

The Business Shoe

The term "business shoe" makes most people think of a black lace-up worn by a banker. But what counts as "business" can encompass far more than just a range of classic shoes for suit-wearers. Many men pursue their profession in shoes that actually belong in their leisure wardrobe, making their selection based on other considerations, of course. The traditional business shoe, however, has to fulfill certain specific criteria in order to convey the wearer's competence, confidence, and ambition, as well as lend a cosmopolitan air, if desired. A business shoe is black, as a rule: black represents seriousness and strictness, and, in the British tradition that has left its mark right across men's fashion, the black shoe represents the City of London and the financial trading that is carried out there; anybody who has

The No. 1 formal shoe: the Oxford with a toecap.

Rarer, but more elegant; the Oxford without a toecap.

The Derby: more sporty and acceptable in black with a suit.

anything to do with money traditionally wears black shoes in Britain.

Brown shoes are associated with rural life and the weekend, but white-collar workers can wear them as well. This tradition has admittedly been forgotten by all but a few, even in England where men still choose to wear a black shoe with a business suit. A black shoe is also the standard option for business attire in the USA and the simple Oxford is the undisputed first choice.

Brogues (or Budapest shoes), slip-ons (loafers), or buckled shoes (Monk straps) are considered as only a second choice to the true business shoe, the Oxford. In addition to black, a dark brown or the oxblood red of cordovan leather are also acceptable, for example on business trips or on a Friday, but when in doubt, black is always the best option. Sandals and sneakers are not acceptable in the office as a rule and flip-flops are right out.

Black shoes with a perforated pattern go well with tweed.

Not good for a conservative look: the buckled shoe.

The penny loafer: too casual for formal occasions.

Shoes for Formal Occasions

Formal attire has been increasing in popularity for a number of years, and men seem once again to be enjoying the idea of honoring an event with the right outfit. However, formal clothes must be appropriate for the occasion and shoes must also match.

Daytime Occasions
DARK SUIT
Shoe: black Oxfords. For festive occasions, black slip-ons or Monk straps will also do. Brogues are generally too sporty.

STRESEMANN (STROLLER SUIT)
Shoe: black Oxfords, plaintip Oxfords.

MORNING DRESS
Shoe: black Oxfords, plaintip Oxfords. For celebratory morning dress occasions, such as weddings, baptisms, or summer parties, also Monk straps. British Sloane Rangers and their impersonators also wear black Gucci loafers with morning dress.

Evening Occasions
BLACK SUIT
Shoe: black lace-ups, slip-ons, Chelsea boots or Monk shoes with an unpatterned finish (also with open lacing, i.e. Derby styles), made from smooth or napped leather.

TUXEDO/WHITE TUXEDO
Shoe: black patent Oxfords, patent leather or fine calfskin evening pumps (polished with water, see page 190), with or without bows. Fine calfskin Oxfords (wingtip or plaintip) buffed to a mirror-like shine are also an option. Satin ribbons may be worn instead of the usual laces in the evening. Black velvet slippers are elegant, but are actually only ever worn with a velvet smoking jacket on domestic occasions.

VELVET SMOKING JACKET
Shoe: velvet slippers in a color to match the jacket, either a similar shade or a complementary contrast (green shoes with a red jacket or vice versa).

TAILS
Shoe: evening dress pumps with bows, black patent Oxfords, mirror-shine Oxfords made from normal calfskin (wingtip or plaintip).

Patent shoes can be worn with a tuxedo. However, they are not suitable for daytime engagements.

Colored velvet pumps were originally worn with a velvet smoking jacket, in a color to match the fabric of the jacket of course.

The plaintip Oxford is a little more formal than the wingtip Oxford and goes with a dark suit, morning dress, or tuxedo.

(Below) Connoisseurs and the bold can combine a tuxedo with dinner dress pumps, with or without the silk bows required for tails.

(Below) Sloane Ranger style: loafers with a snaffle bit to go with a tuxedo (model: Allen Edmonds).

The black Oxford is the all-round shoe for the formal wardrobe, being appropriate for all daytime events and even a possible complement to dinner dress.

Jan-Henrik M. Scheper-Stuke on Shoes

"
Ties and bow ties are my job and

my passion, but all these silk accessories

only look their best when combined with

the right shoes. Shoes and ties belong
"
together like food and wine.

Jan-Henrik M. Scheper-Stuke is the CEO of Edsor Kronen, a Berlin tie manufacturer. Such a dry description is factually correct, but only touches on one aspect of this businessman—he is also a style icon, a popular public speaker, a PR genius, a trendsetter, and an entertainer, not to mention a family man in his private life. Those who have been lucky enough to receive an invitation know him as a generous host, and his collection of shoes is almost as comprehensive as his collection of ties.

Matching Shoes to Outfits

Most people stick to the rules outlined in the previous section for business and leisurewear as well as for formal occasions, even those who choose their clothes based on aesthetic criteria—perhaps in order not to look out of place, or perhaps because they like the accepted outfit combinations. Certain variations on the norms of classic clothing have become firmly entrenched, however, and here Italy led the field in the 1980s, making certain combinations of colors, fabrics, and especially shoes popular all over the world: the stylish northern Italian would happily choose a brown shoe made from smooth or suede leather to go with his light virgin wool suit of anthracite gray.

Those opting for a brown shoe with dark business clothes have a range of classic combinations to choose from: for a start, there is the option just mentioned, of dark brown shoes with a dark gray suit, where a brogue is a popular choice and is equally favored with gray flannel pants and a sport coat or blue blazer. The latter look is a hardy perennial in France, Italy, and Spain. A very light brogue is a far from uncommon choice with gray pants and a blue jacket.

Although a brown suede shoe is in principle just as acceptable worn in combination with a dark suit as a smooth leather brogue, it is more at home in the nebulous region somewhere between business- and leisurewear that is best represented by light cotton pants. These occupy the exact middle ground between the two extremes of "gray flannel pants" and "jeans" and have become extremely popular in this role.

When combining shoes and clothes, always consider the textures of both: a suit in a heavy woolen fabric goes best with shoes made of material with a similar textural structure. Suede, whose texture is wool-like, would fit the bill here, as would smooth leather, if its plain outer surface were supplemented with some textural structure in the form of seams and perforations: a suede loafer would therefore be a good choice with a Glen plaid suit in a heavy winter material, as would a full brogue in black calfskin. The two combinations would be viewed and worn differently depending on the homeland of the fashion-conscious wearer: Glen plaid and suede leather would be a Brit's sporty weekend outfit or the choice of an Italian for a business lunch in the city.

A Glen plaid suit worn accompanied with black full brogues is a business classic in the USA but something of a rarity in the UK, however, where Glen checks are most definitely considered a sporty design.

How do I pick out the right shoes? What footwear goes with what outfit and for what occasion? When do I wear brown or black, and with what colors? These questions can be answered in a number of ways, depending on your priorities. On the one hand you can simply follow the traditional customs and practices that have been established over time; this system could be summed up by saying

simply "that's just how we do things." While another way of making sartorial decisions is based on purely aesthetic appeal, allowing the personal taste of the individual considerably more say in the matter. "I think that looks good" would neatly summarize this approach. The choice of shoes can also be based on other criteria, such as selecting colors, fabrics, and textures based on skin tone, which would be summed up by saying "that suits you because...."

Take the first system—choosing clothes and shoes according to custom and tradition. Most of these sartorial rules have their roots in Britain, the motherland of men's fashion. In the search for

You can buy the shoes to match the suit at a complete outfitter's like Cove & Co.

the right combination of clothing and footwear, there are two sets of dress codes to consider: rural and urban wear, and business- and leisurewear. In an urban environment, you would wear black shoes or brown town shoes for both business and pleasure. Black shoes would be worn with a dark suit and black or brown leisure shoes with leisurewear that has some degree of formality. Leisurewear in town in its most extreme formal incarnation might consist of a business suit with black shoes, while the least formal option would be a shirt, pullover, and jeans with loafers or deck shoes.

The original distinction between dressing for town or country in terms of footwear was that black shoes were always worn in town and brown shoes were reserved for the country; however, brown shoes have come to be acceptable in urban environments over the last three decades. This difference between town and country is of only limited relevance outside the UK, and even the British are now almost entirely unfamiliar with it or, if they are conscious of the rule, fail to follow it.

The concept is nonetheless extremely important for the classification of different kinds of shoes. Once you know that the brown full brogue was originally a shoe for the country and was at best considered a leisure shoe in town, it is easy to see why it does not go so well with a dark business suit. This rule would suggest that black Oxfords, brogues, Monk straps, or loafers would be the shoes of choice for town and therefore also for business. The same shoes in brown are automatically considered leisure shoes in town or formal shoes in the country, with "brown" covering all shades from dark oak to light sandy tones.

If you are looking more subtle distinctions, you could also grade shoes according to their degree of formality, and the basic rule here is that the lace-up is more formal than the slip-on.

Important: brown belt with brown shoes (Photo: Allen Edmonds).

The more foot that is revealed, the more casual the look. Black, ankle-high lace-up boots would be at the absolute top end of the formality scale, while a low-cut loafer would be hovering on the edge of "just about formal." If you accept the rule that a business outfit demands a black shoe, you can still express plenty of individuality in your choice of shoe. The conflicting opinions about the exact place of the loafer in the broad spectrum of shoe shapes falls along national lines: welted loafers are worn in the UK and the USA as part of the classic business look, while Continental Europe favors the lace-up.

Town wear includes three classic formal outfits: "morning dress," "tuxedo," and "tails." Morning dress is worn during the day for very formal occasions—family events like weddings and baptisms, or official occasions such as diplomatic receptions, state funerals, and award ceremonies (as long as they are taking place during the day, of course). Smooth, black Oxfords should always be the shoe of choice, although Monk straps or even loafers can be worn to weddings. Under no circumstances should brogues, and certainly never brown shoes, be worn with morning dress. A tuxedo is designed specifically for evening wear in black or midnight blue, and the custom of wearing it for weddings, which has found widespread favor in some countries, is a strange affectation. The white tuxedo, which has replaced the black jacket at sea or for outdoor occasions, is the only acceptable variation on the tuxedo. Black evening shoes are worn with this, either Oxfords or pumps with silk bows. Tails require these patent leather pumps with bows.

(Above) The choice: matching shoes to fabrics at Cove & Co. (Below) The devil is in the detail: Allen Edmonds sells woven belts to match their loafers.

It's All in the Mix!

The composition of most men's shoe racks is determined by their profession: a banker needs plenty of black classics, although dark brown shoes have been finding their way into the financial sector. An art director will often be seen running around the office, or even the client's office, in sneakers, while a landscape architect will wear boots, for practical reasons if nothing else.

But there is more to life than work—when a banker goes out for a beer in the

Smart casual: jeans, sport coat, welted shoes.

Summer business attire: cotton suit,

evening, he leaves the black Oxfords in the wardrobe and pulls on his lumberjack boots. A graphic designer will turn to brown chukka boots for a date and team them with chinos and a sport coat; a landscape gardener will change into fine lace-ups or even patent leather pumps with a suit for the evening.

You need the right shoes for work and the right shoes for leisure, and the relationship between the two—footwear for the office and shoes worn for leisure in the evenings and at weekends—has to be decided on an individual basis.

However, the tendency today is toward dress codes that are less and less prescriptive—men have more free time and are therefore wearing shoes that are more casual in style.

woven lace-ups.

Office attire: brown loafers, pinstripe suit. (All photos: Allen Edmonds.)

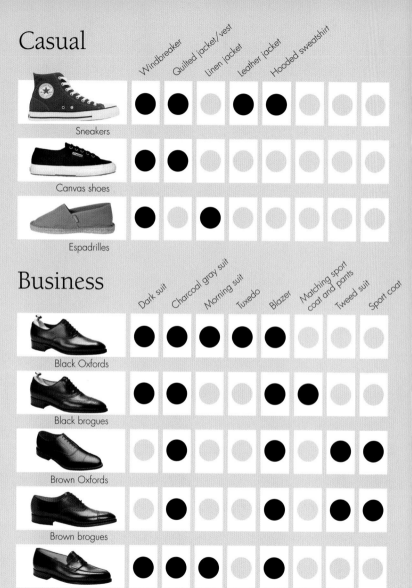

Casual

	Windbreaker	Quilted jacket/vest	Linen jacket	Leather jacket	Hooded sweatshirt
Sneakers	●	●	○	●	●
Canvas shoes	●	●	○	○	○
Espadrilles	●	○	●	○	○

Business

	Dark suit	Charcoal gray suit	Morning suit	Tuxedo	Blazer	Matching sport coat and pants	Tweed suit	Sport coat
Black Oxfords	●	●	●	●	●	○	○	○
Black brogues	●	●	○	○	●	●	○	○
Brown Oxfords	○	●	○	○	●	○	●	●
Brown brogues	○	●	○	○	●	○	●	●
Black loafers	●	●	●	○	●	○	○	○

Smart Casual

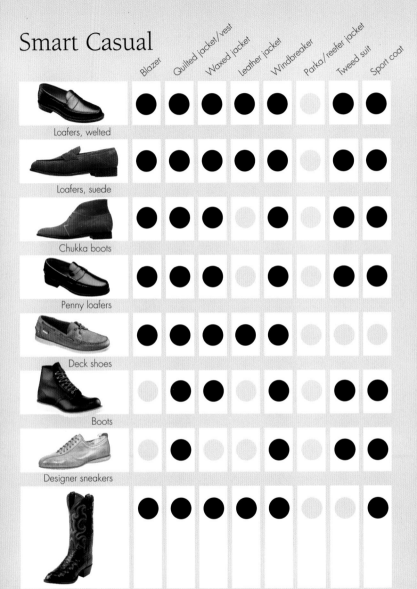

	Blazer	Quilted jacket/vest	Waxed jacket	Leather jacket	Windbreaker	Parka/reefer jacket	Tweed suit	Sport coat
Loafers, welted	●	●	●	●	●	○	●	●
Loafers, suede	●	●	●	●	●	○	●	●
Chukka boots	●	●	●	○	●	○	●	●
Penny loafers	●	●	●	○	●	○	●	●
Deck shoes	●	●	●	●	●	○	○	○
Boots	○	●	●	○	●	○	●	●
Designer sneakers	○	●	○	○	●	○	●	●
Cowboy boots	●	●	●	●	●	○	○	●

Socks

Socks are an essential part of the overall look of an outfit. The basic rules are as follows: black, dark gray, or dark blue knee socks are correct with business shoes, while colors and patterns are only permissable for leisurewear. White socks have been anathema for some time, and rightly so, if they are toweling socks bought in a six-pack; a white knee sock in fine cotton or silk would be a better choice, although only to go with clothing that is very light in color, with light brown or white shoes. If you feel confident enough to don two-tone spectator shoes or saddle-shoe Oxfords, you may also risk white socks. In addition to the functional choices, there are of course other options when choosing a sock for business: red socks would be a conceivable alternative with a dark blue suit,

light blue shirt, and a dark blue tie with white polka dots.

And if the socks were the same color as the silk handkerchief in your breast pocket, the result would be stylish in the extreme. However, colored socks should always attract a red flag, as it were, if a dark suit is to be worn for a truly solemn occasion; to what extent work should count as a solemn occasion is up to the individual, but it is at best unlikely that emerald green socks are appropriate for, say, a board meeting at a bank. Black knee socks are decidedly the least adventurous but also the most reliable option. Fans of colored socks can let their imaginations run riot when teamed with leisurewear, when black socks would as a rule be too stark a contrast with colors often worn at the weekend. Socks of more varied hues would blend more harmoniously with an outfit in tweed, corduroy, cotton, or wool. Burgundy, bottle green, or even brown have become quite popular, but similarly we should not shy away from red, yellow, or light blue when work ends on a Friday. Striped or Argyle pattern socks are also entirely appropriate for free time.

Robert Petrović on Shoes

" *For me, shoes are not merely a fashion object; apart from the fact that shoes have been my constant companions as I make my way through the 21st century, they are also a reflection of my innermost self. To my mind, a glance at someone's shoes can give much away—whether they are expensive, colorful, or vintage:* " *shoes betray the character of a person.*

Robert Petrović is manager of the Ritz Carlton on Potsdamer Platz in Berlin. Born in Vienna, he sees himself as the head servant of his guests, who, true to the hotel's motto, are waited on by "ladies and gentlemen."

Questions

QUESTION: Is there a rule of thumb for choosing the right shoes for an outfit?

ANSWER: There are two basic rules. The shoes should either blend in harmoniously or provide a contrast; so you can wear sneakers with jeans or sneakers with a suit. Shoes should always be appropriate to the occasion. Most people are not bothered by how they look during their leisure time but at a silver wedding anniversary you should take the hosts' expectations into consideration.

QUESTION: Do I have to wear special shoes with a tuxedo?

ANSWER: As a tuxedo is a form of evening dress, it requires evening shoes. If you are not keen on making the investment or are only renting the tux, you can combine it with black Oxfords (with or without wingtips) as an exception, but these must be polished to a perfect shine. Shoes with perforations in a brogue style should never be worn with a tuxedo. Evening shoes, such as pumps, are required with tails, however, while a velvet smoking jacket is teamed with velvet slippers, which may match the color of the jacket.

QUESTION: Can I wear my patent leather shoes to the office as well?

ANSWER: It depends on what job you do in the office. Black patent leather shoes are traditionally reserved for evening wear and a gentleman wears them only with a tuxedo or tails, although they are also found in a range of colors in designer fashion. They should definitely be avoided in a conservative work environment, but if things are casual or there is no dress code, a fashion victim should have free reign.

QUESTION: You often see people wearing Gucci loafers with a snaffle bit with a tuxedo or morning dress in the UK. Is that really on?

ANSWER: Gucci loafers are part of the so-called Sloane Ranger look sported by members of the British middle and upper classes. While extremely English and classic, the look also favors strong color contrasts (such as red socks with a dark blue suit or light blue cords with a tweed sport coat). Sloane Rangers will wear Gucci loafers at the drop of a hat and will also combine the black model with a tuxedo. As no one else would dream of wearing such shoes with evening dress, you should consider carefully whether you can pull such a look off. If you wish to go down a more traditional route, choose evening shoes with a tux, and Oxfords with or without a toecap with morning dress.

& Answers

QUESTION: Can I wear colored socks in the office?

ANSWER: The answer here is also dependent on what sector you work in, and the job that you do also makes a difference: the head of a law firm or a real estate broker specializing in luxury apartments may indeed wear Burgundy, bottle green, or even mauve socks with a suit, but a group of bankers would regard colored socks with suspicion. You are free to choose your sock color and design in sectors where there is no dress code, of course.

QUESTION: Which criteria should I follow to choose the color of my socks? To match the suit or the shoes?

ANSWER: The socks must match both suit and shoes. For formal occasions or in a traditional business setting, select dark socks (dark gray, black, navy blue) with black or dark brown shoes, but colored socks are an attractive option with sporty suits.

QUESTION: What sock color would be suitable for wearing with black shoes and a dark blue suit?

ANSWER: Combining black and dark blue is often thought a no-no, especially by young men. There are traditionally only two options when wearing black shoes with a dark blue suit: black or dark blue socks.

QUESTION: Do loafers go with a suit?

ANSWER: Until the First World War, the formal men's shoe of choice was the low boot and the half-shoe was considered, literally, not to be "full" footwear. The closest cousin of the laced low boot is the lace-up shoe like the Oxford. Traditionalists regard it as the most formal and often only permissible option to wear with a suit. Others are not quite so strict and will consider other lace-up styles. Slip-on shoes such as loafers may be regarded as too sporty, however (a view widespread across Continental Europe), although welted slip-ons have been worn with suits—if only as daywear—in the UK and USA since the 1930s. Lace-ups remain the best choice for formal occasions and evening wear.

QUESTION: Are white socks really that bad with a suit?

ANSWER: White silk or cotton socks would not be unusual with a white linen suit and white shoes, but packs of cheap white socks are an absolute no-no with black shoes. Fortunately this is rarely seen these days. Short black socks with a suit would be almost as bad; formal outfits require knee socks, even in summer.

Glossary

A

AGO Actually a term describing an adhesive, developed in 1910, with which the sole is attached to the upper; refers to the glued styles of manufacture, as opposed to the stitched styles of manufacture.

B

Balmoral Another term for the Oxford style with a laced front.

Bal-type Describes shoes with closed lacing.

Beef roll An American style of slip-on, similar in shape to a penny loafer.

Bespoke shoes Shoes that have been custom-made for a particular individual. Generally refers to handmade, welted shoes.

Blake Describes the through-stitched manufacturing style that was named for the inventor of the machine used (*see* Through-stitched).

Blucher American expression for a shoe with open lacing. The quarter panels of the shoe are sewn onto the upper. The vamp, the part of the shoe covering the instep and toes, connects seamlessly to the tongue.

Box calf Calfskin.

Braided welt A decorative stitch for double-stitched shoes.

Brogues Shoes with decorative perforations arranged in the shape of a lyre.

Budapest Wingtip shoes, a common name for a version of the British brogue manufactured in Hungary (*see* Brogues).

C

Chaps Gaiters reaching the knee, worn over low boots by riders for protection. Fur-lined chaps can be used in winter.

Chelsea boots Ankle-high boots with elasticized panels on the side.

Chrome tanning Tanning with chrome salts; the most common kind of tanning for leather used to make shoe uppers.

Chukka boots Ankle-height boots made of brown suede leather, generally with a leather sole.

College shoes *See* Penny loafers.

Cordovan Another expression for equine leather; a rare and expensive raw material for shoes. The leather suitable for shoes is taken from the horse's hindquarters and provides two round pieces of hide that are sufficient for two or three pairs.

Cork cushioning Cork is inserted beneath the inner sole in welted shoes to help absorb the impact of walking. The foot makes an impression in the cork known as the footbed.

D

Deck shoes Moccasins made from polished leather with leather laces and a non-slip plastic sole.

Derby A shoe with open lacing (*see also* Blucher).

Double-stitched A variant of the welted manufacturing style in which a seam connects the upper to the inner sole and the welt is sewn to the upper, which is bent out. The outer sole is then (double-)stitched to the welt. Typical style for hiking and climbing boots.

Doubling Sewing the outer sole to the welt.

Driving shoes Slip-ons with a nonslip, profiled sole that reaches up over the heel. Intended to prevent the foot slipping when operating the pedals.

E

Escarpin Low pumps for men, often with a black bow, traditionally worn with tails and occasionally with a tuxedo.

F

Flexible stitching Manufacturing style in which the upper is bent outward and sewn to the inner and outer sole.

G

Gaiters Protective covering for the foot, ankle, or calf, made from waterproof fabric or leather. Gaiters are wrapped round the leg and attached with straps or buckles. Gaiters are often additionally held in place by a loop that sits in front of the heel of the shoe.

Galoshes Rubber overshoes to protect footwear and feet from water and cold, and to prevent slipping.

Goodyear method Another term for the factory manufacture of welted shoes using the sewing machine, patented by Charles Goodyear in the 19th century.

Goyser A double-stitched mountain boot invented in Bad Goisern in Austria.

H

Haferl shoes Double-stitched, low work shoes or walking shoes with central or side laces, commonly found in the Alpine regions of Germany and Austria. Originally made with a leather sole, now mostly featuring a molded rubber sole.

I

Inner sole The inner sole of the shoe.

Insole lip A section channeled into the inner sole through which the upper and the welt are stitched together when manufacturing welted shoes (*see* Rib).

J

Jodhpur boots A slightly taller than ankle-height riding boot with a buckle closure and leather sole. Also popular worn as a leisure shoe.

L

Last A simplified reproduction of the human foot, constructed to average dimensions for factory-made shoes and to the measurements of the client for bespoke shoes. A handmade last is carved from wood and the shoe is built up around it.

Locherl shoes Summer half-shoes with perforations in the upper to increase breathability.

Lyre perforations A style of decorative pattern in which the holes in brogues and Budapest shoes are arranged.

M

McKay Term describing the through-stitched manufacturing process (*see* Through-stitched *and* Blake).

Moccasins Footwear originating with Native Americans, now any shoe where the upper is drawn up around the last from beneath. Gucci loafers and deck shoes are moccasin-style shoes (*see also* Opanka).

Monk straps Unlaced shoes fastened with a buckle.

N

Norwegian Sporty men's Derby-style shoe with an inset vamp and a vertical seam at the toe. Frequently worn with a rubber molded sole in bad weather, less often as an ankle-boot.

O

Opanka One of the most ancient styles of shoe, similar in construction to a moccasin.

Ostrich leather Ostrich skin has certain characteristics suiting it to the manufacture of small leather articles such as wallets or watchstraps, but it is also used to make shoes.

Oxford The most formal men's shoe to wear with a suit, with closed lacing and a plain toecap. The plaintip Oxford, with no toecap, is similarly formal.

P

Paddock boots Ankle boots with elasticized sidings for equestrian sports.

Patent leather A coated, high-gloss leather. Traditionally worn only with evening dress, but also used by designers for day shoes.

Penny loafers A moccasin-style slip-on that was originally through-stitched. The name comes from the coin that was once placed under the strap to bring luck. Also known as college shoes.

Plaintip An Oxford with no toecap (*see also* Oxford).

Pumps Low-cut, low-heeled evening shoes made from, for example, patent leather. Worn with tails, smoking jacket, or a tuxedo, and once exclusively men's shoes (*see also* Escarpin).

R

Rib A narrow strip of leather glued underneath the inner sole in welted shoes. The welt and upper are sewn to the inner sole through the rib.

Russia leather Vegetable-tanned calfskin or cattle leather. Soft, thick, and originally produced in Russia, it is treated with birch tar oil to make it waterproof.

S

Saddle shoes Shoes with closed lacing whereby the side parts of the vamp sit across the instep like a saddle. The saddle is usually a different color from the leather for the rest of the upper. A style also popular as a golf shoe.

Shank A long strip of metal placed under the footbed to provide stability; it is to be found within the cork padding between the inner and outer sole and may be made of other materials.

Shoe tree A foot-shaped device made of wood or plastic that is placed inside the shoe to exert pressure when it is not being worn. Helps to ensure the leather retains its shape.

Slip-ons Another term for loafers.

Slippers British term for babouches or house shoes. Also used by the British to describe some loafers, or "slip-ons."

Spectator shoes Two-tone shoes (typically brown, black, or blue paired with white), e.g. a brogue in which the toecap has a different color from the other sections of the upper.

Stitching Sewing together the sections of a shoe's upper.

Stormwelt A narrow strip of leather inserted between the welt and upper to prevent the intrusion of water, such as is found in golf shoes.

T

Tacking After the upper has been stretched over the last, it is temporarily attached to the inner sole with little nails.

Tasseled loafers Slip-on shoes with ornamental tassels. A loafer in which the laces are threaded round the shoe through eyes or "tunnels" and then tied at the instep in the form of a bow. The ends of the laces are decorated with tassels. The first such shoe was a tasseled loafer made by Alden.

Through-stitched A method of manufacturing light lace-ups and slip-ons whereby the upper, inner sole, and outer sole are sewn together with a single seam. Also known as the Blake method.

Trunk show Derived from the "trunk" used for travel and storage; a sales event in which usually tailors, shirtmakers, or shoemakers present their wares and take orders in hotels or elsewhere.

U

Upper The top section of the shoe, as opposed to the sole.

V

Vamp The front part of the shoe and/or upper.

Veldtschoen A method of manufacturing welted shoes in which the leather of the upper is bent out before being stitched to the welt. Said to make the shoe waterproof. Used for tough hiking or hunting boots.

W

Wedge heel A shoe in which the sole and heel are made in one piece and grow thicker toward the heel.

Wellington boots, Wellingtons, Wellies British terms for gum boots.

Welted A complicated manufacturing style, at least for men's shoes, in which the upper, the welt, and the inner sole are connected with one seam; the outer sole is then (double-) stitched to the welt, either by hand or using a machine (*see also* Goodyear method).

Wingtip Curved toecap for men's shoes. A shoe with a wingtip is known as a brogue or a Budapest shoe.

Index

Picture Credits

c=center, r=right, l=left, a=above, b=below
fr=from

© adidas AG, Herzogenaurach: 111, 120 a., 124 b., 126 a., 127 a., 132, 133, 143
© A. Königs GmbH, Erkelenz-Tenholt: 144–147
© Alden Shoe Company, Middleborough: 54, 209 a.
© Allen Edmonds Shoe Corporation, Port Washington: 20 b.r., 21 (2nd fr. a.), 102 (3rd and 4th fr. a.), 130, 136, 137, 139, 184 c., 185 a.l., 185 c.l., 185 b., 189 a., 189 c., 196, 197, 211 b.c., 216, 217 b., 218, 219, 220 (3rd fr. b.), 221 (1st and 4th fr. a.)
© Asics Corporation, Kobe: 121 a., 125 a., 134, 135
© Bernhard Roetzel, Berlin: 160, 162–165, 176, 177, 206
© Birkenstock Orthopädie GmbH & Co. KG, Vettelschoss: 23 (3rd fr. a.), 103 b., 105 a.l., 105 b.r., 108, 109
© Brütting & Co. EB-Sport International GmbH, Küps: 142
© Burgol®, Freyersfeld Vertriebsgesellschaft mbH, Constance: 180, 181, 184 a., 184 b., 185 a.l., 185 c.r., 190, 191, 194, 195, 228 c.
© Catrin Moritz, Essen, for Falke KGaA, Schmallenberg: 58
© Clarks International, Somerset: 20 c.l., 23 b., 52/53
© Converse Inc.: 9 a., 22 (3rd fr. a.), 22 b.r., 56, 57, 103 a., 120 b., 125 b., 220 (1st fr. a.), 228 a.l.
© Cove & Co., Düsseldorf: 8/9 b., 44, 66/67, 210, 211 c.a., 215, 217 a., 222/223
© Crockett & Jones, Northampton: 46, 47, 48, 49 a.l., 51 a., 61, 74, 75, 104 a.r., 104 b.l., 179, 211 a.l., 211 b.l., 211 a.r., 228 a.r. and c.
© Dieter Kuckelkorn / Anneliese Kuckelkorn GmbH & Co. KG, Aachen: 103 (3rd fr. a.), 106 b.

© Dr. Martens AirWay International, Northants: 21 b.r., 22 a.l., 22 (2nd fr. a.), 23 a.l.
© Eduard Meier, Munich: 28, 29, 31, 49 b.r., 50, 65, 72, 94, 95, 102 b., 138, 174, 183, 187, 202 a.l., 202 b.l., 208, 209 b.
© erill.fritz.fotografien.: 6, 30, 34, 35, 40, 41, 51 c., 51 b., 62, 63, 105 a.r., 118, 192, 193, 198–201, 202 c., 202 a.r., 202 b.r., 203, 211 b.r., 220 (4th and 5. fr. a.), 220 (1st and 2nd fr. b.), 228 b.r. and b.l.
© [espadrij] l'originale/Panorama Europe GmbH, Düsseldorf: 102 (2nd fr. a.), 105 b.l., 114, 115, 220 (3rd fr. a.)
© Ethan Amos Newton for Saint Crispin's, Vienna: 70
© Fender Musical Instruments GmbH, Düsseldorf: 18
© Giesswein Walkwaren AG, Brixlegg: 104 a.l., 104 b.r.
© HAFLINGER, iesse-Schuh GmbH, Goslar: 103 (2nd fr. a.)
© HANWAG GmbH, Vierkirchen-Pasenbach: 39, 149, 150 b., 150 (2nd fr. a.), 151 c.
© Havaianas/Alpargatas S.A., Sao Paulo: 21 a., 110
© Heinrich Dinkelacker GmbH, Bietigheim-Bissingen: 38 (2nd fr. a.), 186
© Horween Leather Company, Chicago: 32, 33 a.
© J Barbour & Sons Ltd., South Shields: 152, 159
© John Lobb, London: 88
© Jörg Rausch, www.leder-infa.de: 33 b.
© Kay Blaschke, Munich, for Franz Baron Schoemakers, Munich: 26
© Künzli – SwissShoe AG, Windisch: 15
© Ludwig Reiter Schuhmanufaktur GmbH, Vienna: 73, 107, 124 a., 155 a.r.
© Lukas Meindl GmbH & Co. KG, Kirchanschöring: 38 (except 2nd fr. a.), 148, 150 a., 150 (3rd fr. a.), 151 a., 151 b., 155 a.l., 155 b.l.

© Maison Corthay Paris: 82–85
© Markus Ewers, Berlin, for Ace Jeans: 19
© Michalsky Holding GmbH, Berlin: 122
© New Balance Athletic Shoe, Inc., Boston: 126 b.
© Nokian Footwear, Nokia: 156, 157, 158, 161
© Orion Dahlmann, Düsseldorf, for Ignatious Joseph, Düsseldorf: 96
© picture-alliance / akg-images: 10, 24, 25
© PRIME SHOES GmbH, Greifenberg/Munich: 155 b.r.
© PUMA SE, Herzogenaurach: 121 b.
© Red Wing Shoe Company, Red Wing: 21 (3rd fr. a.), 154 a.r., 154 b.l., 221 (3rd fr. b.)
© Reiner Bajo, Berlin: 16
© Rivieras Leisure Shoes, Paris: 112, 113
© Santoni, Milan: 128 a.
© Scabal SA, Brussels: 92
© SEBAGO®, Michigan: 100, 102 a., 178, 220 (2nd fr. a.), 221 (4th fr. b.)
© SHOEPASSION, Berlin: 14, 36, 37, 188, 189 b., 228 b.c.
© Starpix/Tuma: 86
© Teva®, Deckers Consumer Direct Corporation: 23 (2nd fr. a.), 106
© The Ritz Carlton, Berlin: 224
© The Timberland World Trading GmbH, Munich: 154 a.l.
© Thomas Rabsch, Cologne, for Cove & Co., Düsseldorf: 140
© Tina Linster for Edsor Kronen, Berlin: 212
© Tony Lama Boots: 20 a.r., 168–171, 221 (1st fr. b.), 228 c.
© Tricker's, R.E. Tricker Ltd, Northampton: 55, 103 (4th fr. a.), 154 b.r., 166, 167, 221 (2nd and 3rd fr. a.), 211 c. (2nd fr. b.), 228 c.a. and c.r.
© Vickermann & Stoya, Baden-Baden: 76, 77, 91, 129, 220 (2nd fr. b.)
© Wikipedia.org/Photo: Kevin Vertucio, Yardley, PA: 127 b.